A Decade of Cameroon

A Decade of Cameroon

Politics, Economy and Society 2008–2017

By

Fanny Pigeaud

BRILL

LEIDEN | BOSTON

Library of Congress Cataloging-in-Publication Data

Names: Pigeaud, Fanny, author.
Title: A decade of Cameroon : politics, economy and society 2008–2017 / by
   Fanny Pigeaud.
Description: Boston : Brill, 2019.
Identifiers: LCCN 2019014070 (print) | LCCN 2019015031 (ebook) |
   ISBN 9789004401532 (ebook) | ISBN 9789004395251 (pbk. : alk. paper)
Subjects: LCSH: Cameroon—Politics and government—21st century. |
   Cameroon—Economic conditions—21st century. | Cameroon—Social
   conditions—21st century.
Classification: LCC DT578 (ebook) | LCC DT578 .P543 2019 (print) |
   DDC 967.11042—dc23
LC record available at https://lccn.loc.gov/2019014070

Typeface for the Latin, Greek, and Cyrillic scripts: "Brill". See and download: brill.com/
brill-typeface.

ISBN 978-90-04-39525-1 (paperback)
ISBN 978-90-04-40153-2 (e-book)

This book is printed on acid-free paper and produced in a sustainable manner.

Printed by Printforce, United Kingdom

Contents

Cameroon in 2008

Violence erupted at the beginning of the year as a result of both economic and political grievances, rocking a country usually described as the most peaceful in Central Africa. After a bout of harsh repression and a number of economic measures meant to improve the purchasing power of Cameroonians, the National Assembly eventually approved the controversial constitutional amendment removing the two-term limit on the presidency. This move occurred during a year also marked by tense relations with some neighbouring countries. Attacks on Cameroonian troops, especially in the Bakassi peninsula, which was eventually transferred from Nigerian control, repeatedly threatened the country's security.

Domestic Politics

In November 2007, the 25th anniversary celebrations of the Biya regime triggered a large increase in the notorious 'motions of support' for the head of state. Officials of the ruling 'Rassemblement Démocratique du Peuple Camerounais' (RDPC), publicly announced their support for a *constitutional amendment* to remove the two-term limit on the presidency. In his nationwide end-of-the-year address on 31 December 2007, Paul Biya himself argued that such constitutional limitation was inconsistent with the very idea of democratic choice. This statement set off a wave of protests led by the Social Democratic Front (SDF), the main opposition party. Public demonstrations against the constitutional amendment were held in Douala on 14 and 23 February, despite a ban imposed in mid-January on public meetings and demonstrations in Littoral province. Both demonstrations were followed by violent repression. On 25 February, *road hauliers went on strike* against the increase in the

© KONINKLIJKE BRILL NV, LEIDEN, 2019 | DOI:10.1163/9789004401532_002

prices of fuel and basic goods. Violence erupted in Douala and in
other towns in the western provinces, where shops were closed and
traffic halted. In the streets, people demonstrated against the loss
of purchasing power and the proposed constitutional amendment,
which was interpreted as a way for the president to remain in power
after 2011. The strike ended after the price of fuel was reduced on
27 February, but violence continued in the major cities, where gangs
of young men looted shops and fuel stations. In a TV address on this
day, President Paul Biya implicitly accused opposition parties of
manipulating the young rioters. There were a number of incidents
reported in Yaoundé, especially at the university, following the deployment of armed forces. The riots abated at the end of this turbu-
lent week. The president announced on 7 March a tariff reduction
on imported basic goods. The government also promised to increase
the salaries of civil servants by 15%. Later in the month, the price of
electricity was also reduced.

The number of casualties in the riots and the *repression* became a matter of debate. On one hand, the 'Maison des Droits de
l'Homme', a human rights NGO based in Douala, stated that more
than 100 people had been killed, while on the other, the government
acknowledged that only 40 had died during the February riots. The
suppression of these demonstrations and riots was accompanied by
measures against the private press. In January, Equinoxe TV, a private channel, was closed, officially for non-payment of the registration tax, while a month later, Magic FM, a private radio station, had
its equipment confiscated. Both measures against the media could
be interpreted as being intended to prevent public criticism of the
government's handling of the crisis. This curtailment of freedom of
expression and the ban on public demonstrations in Douala were
lifted only in July.

In the meantime, parliament voted in the controversial constitutional amendment by a large majority (157 in favour, 5 opposed
and 15 abstentions). The opposition parties denounced the fact that
the vote was brought forward without prior notice. The main con-

stitutional amendment was *the removal of the two-term limit on the presidential mandate.* While less remarked upon, the amendment of article 53 was also important: a new clause in the constitution states that the activities of the president will enjoy immunity, which would continue beyond the end of his mandate. The SDF was vocal in condemning the constitutional amendment but, with only 15 representatives in the National Assembly, could not effectively oppose it. Moreover, John Fru Ndi, the chairman of the party, still faced charges of murdering a SDF member, but his trial was postponed twice during the year. About 20 other members of the SDF involved in the same case and detained without trial since 2006 were released in November.

The SDF also opposed the nomination of the members of Elections Cameroon (ELECAM), the new institution responsible for organising and supervising elections. On 30 December, President Biya nominated its 12 members, 11 of whom were either members of the central committee or the political bureau of the RDPC or close allies of the executive. This new institution had been created by law in 2006 and its mandate was formerly jointly discharged by the interior ministry and the 'Observatoire National des Elections' (ONEL).

The government continued with its *anti-corruption campaign.* Specifically, the 'Epervier' operation entered its second phase. In March, two prominent former ministers, Polycarpe Abah Abah, former minister of finance and Urbain Olanguena Awono, former minister of health, as well as several high-ranking officials in state agencies were arrested for the large-scale embezzlement of public funds. In April, Jean Marie Atangana Mebara, former secretary general of the presidency, was interrogated by police about the controversial purchase of a presidential aircraft and was arrested in August. Several other former ministers and heads of administration were dismissed, tried or arrested during the year on allegations of corruption. Some of the individuals arrested during the first phase of the anti-corruption campaign, which started in 2006, were sentenced to from 20 to 40 years of imprisonment. Accusations of corruption were particularly common in the forestry sector. In April, a retired forester published a report detailing the corrupt practices in the sector. According to donors, corruption in the forestry sector amounted to a yearly loss to the state budget of tens of millions of euros. Minister of Forests and Fauna Elvis Ngolle Ngolle acknowledged that persistent problems threatened the sector and withdrew the licences of a dozen small forestry firms. However, when the French branch of Friends of the Earth, an international NGO, issued a second report on the matter in June, Ngolle Ngolle claimed that the sector was now a "model of good governance". Corruption was also stated to be rampant in the *agricultural sector*: the 'Association Citoyenne de Défense des Intérêts Collectifs' (ACDIC) published a report in December highlighting the embezzlement of foreign aid in this sector. According to ACDIC, in 2008 € 1.8 m was poured in to support the production of maize. However, 62% of the funding had been misappropriated by civil servants in the ministry of agriculture. The publicity surrounding the report led in December to the arrest of the chairman Bernard Njonga and several members of the NGO.

Because of the political and social tensions, *human rights* in the country remained a matter of concern. As noted earlier, public demonstrations in Douala were restricted and the media was muzzled during the first half of the year. The repression of the riots was violent and about 1,600 persons were arrested on charges of public disorder and destruction of private and government property. The minister of justice claimed in April that 729 persons had been fined and/or given prison sentences of from three months to six years. Lawyers and human rights advocates in Cameroon expressed concern that the trials were unusually hasty and unfair. On the national holiday (20 May), Biya decreed a conditional amnesty for prisoners but several dozen prisoners remained in custody, either because they had appealed their convictions and sentences or because they had been unable to pay the fines imposed by the courts. The famous singer Pierre Roger Lambo Sandjo, better known by his pseudonym Lapiro de Mbanga, was arrested in April for his alleged participation in the riots. In September, he was charged with looting and sentenced to three years imprisonment. *Prison conditions* were still harsh and characterised by inadequate food and medical care as well as overcrowding. At least 10 detainees died and as many as 78 sustained injuries after a fire broke out at New Bell prison (Douala) on 20 August. As revealed by a search conducted in August in the same prison after prison authorities were alerted to a massive escape plot, criminality appeared to be on the increase inside prisons, with convicts having easy access to weapons. Attempts at escape had already occurred earlier in the year, and the reaction was harsh: on the afternoon of 29 June, dozens of prisoners forced their way out of New Bell prison and 15 were reportedly shot dead by prison guards and other security forces in the ensuing manhunt. Two others were killed on 30 June.

Domestic insecurity appeared to be on the increase, especially during the second part of the year. Ten persons were abducted in June by bandits in the Extreme-North province and were found dead some days later. Again in October, November and December, attacks by bandits were frequent in the northern provinces but also in the West and Central provinces. Bandits and armed forces were killed in the exchange of fire. The insecurity was also evidenced in the hold-up of three banks in Limbe on the night of 28 September. Heavily armed commando-style groups descended on Limbe by boat and took control of the town for several hours before disappearing.

A continuing worry for the Biya regime was the determined struggle of the *anglophone secessionist movement* to establish an independent state in anglophone Cameroon, the former British trust territory of Southern Cameroons. On 6 October, the chairman and 22 members of the Southern Cameroons National Council (SCNC) were detained for four days for holding an illegal meeting. Members of the SCNC are regularly arrested in early October each year when they celebrate the contested referendum that led to the incorporation of Southern Cameroons into the former French colony.

In August, President Biya created a seventh public *university*, which will be established for the next academic year in the city of Maroua in the Extreme North province, one of the most heavily populated provinces in the country. This institution had been promised by him during the presidential campaigns of 1997 and 2004. It is supposed to relieve the overcrowding in the current university system: no work has ever been undertaken to increase the size of the universities of Yaoundé I and II, Buea (South West), Douala (Littoral), Dschang (West) and Ngadoundéré (North). As in previous years, students and professors continued to complain about their working conditions. For the first time, a student union, the 'Association pour la Défense des Droits des Étudiants du Cameroun' (ADDEC), supported by an NGO, decided in July to lodge a complaint against the director of the public university of journalism 'l'Ecole supérieure des sciences et techniques de l'information et de la communication' of Yaoundé for 'misappropriation': the students accused him of charging illegally high registration fees (CFAfr 600,000 instead of CFAfr 50,000). In November, the main higher education union, the 'Syndicat National des Enseignants du Supérieur', went on strike for five days demanding better salaries. It claimed that the gradual increases the government had promised in 2001 had not been implemented.

Foreign Affairs

The potentially oil-rich *Bakassi peninsula*, bordering Nigeria, was the major concern during the second half of the year. Violence had already erupted in November 2007 with the attack by unidentified assailants on a Cameroonian military post and the death of 21 Cameroonian soldiers. On 9 June, according to Cameroonian authorities, an unidentified armed group kidnapped a divisional officer of Bakassi and five soldiers aboard a pirogue on the Akwa Yafé river bordering Nigeria. All of them were found dead among the

Bakassi mangroves a week later. On 13 July, three soldiers were killed in the same area. A few days after, an unknown Nigerian group, the Bakassi Freedom Fighters (BFF), part of the shadowy Niger Delta Defence and Security Council (NDDSC), claimed responsibility for these armed incidents. It promised new attacks, requested talks with the Cameroonian government on the status of the peninsula and demanded compensation for the forthcoming transfer of the territory held by Nigeria to Cameroon. When the Cameroonian authorities did not respond, BFF killed two soldiers in a new assault on 24 July. Despite the violence and insecurity, Nigeria completely withdrew from the Bakassi peninsula on 14 August in accordance with the 2006 Greentree Agreement, bringing an end to the 15-year dispute over the zone. UN Secretary General Ban Ki-moon described the transfer as "a model for negotiated settlements of border disputes." However, on 31 October, 10 of the 15 crew members on a French oil vessel were kidnapped off the coast of the Bakassi peninsula by BFF gunmen. The motives of the militia were again unclear. After 12 days of detention on Bakassi peninsula, probably on the Nigerian side, the 10 hostages (seven French nationals, one Tunisian and two Cameroonians) were finally exchanged against the release of 13 prisoners. As with the previous attacks, the authorities remained silent and gave no public explanation. The government merely announced that two high-ranking army officers in charge of security in the Bakassi maritime area had been dismissed. However, some military and government sources suggested BFF was involved in arms and ammunition trafficking with high-ranking Cameroonian army officers before the handover. After the hostage crisis, additional troops were sent to protect the Bakassi peninsula.

As in 2007, Cameroon's relations with *Equatorial Guinea* were under stress. In October, the media reported a major scandal involving two Cameroonian police officers and authorities in the neighbouring country. They were accused of having arranged the kidnapping in Yaoundé of an opponent of the regime of President Obiang of Equatorial Guinea. The office of UNHCR protested to the

Cameroonian authorities as the victim, Cipriano Nguema Mba, a former army officer who had been sentenced in 2005 to 30 years imprisonment for a coup attempt, had been granted refugee status in Cameroon. Reports from Equatorial Guinea a few days later indicated the former officer was now detained in the notorious Black Beach prison in Malabo. In November, the two Cameroonian policemen who kidnapped Mba for money and handed him over to the intelligence services of Equatorial Guinea, were arrested, dismissed from the police – a very uncommon occurrence in Cameroon – and charged with collusion with a foreign secret intelligence service by a military court in Cameroon. Cameroonian media reported that the ambassador of Equatorial Guinea had also been summoned to the Cameroonian ministry of foreign affairs, but no further details were disclosed.

Cameroon had also to deal with the aftermath of the troubles of 2–3 February in *Chad*. About 20,000 people, according to humanitarian sources, fled to Cameroon after the failed rebel attack on N'Djaména. A large refugee camp had to be established by the UNHCR near Maltam, a city in the north of the country about 20 kms from the Chadian capital. In April, because of security threats to the refugees, the camp had to be relocated near Garoua, about 350 km to the south. A few weeks earlier, in March, Cameroon had welcomed the Chadian opposition leader Ngarlejy Yorongar for three days in Yaoundé before his departure to France. He had been secretly evacuated from Chad by UNHCR. However, Cameroonian authorities made no public statement about his presence in the country.

In April, UNHCR also reported that dozens of refugees were arriving each month from the western region of the *Central African Republic* to escape bandits and to settle permanently in Cameroon (mostly in the eastern region). According to UNHCR, this flow had begun in 2005 and the number of people involved would soon exceed 50,000.

In June, Cameroon hosted the annual summit of the sub-regional organisation, CEMAC. On that occasion, CEMAC heads of state condemned the persistent rebel attacks against Chad. In 2008, Cameroon was the only CEMAC member to agree to ratify the EPA with the EU, since the European Commission had failed to persuade other countries to sign. Consequently, the Cameroonian government was criticised by private companies and NGOs of the sub-region of breaking sub-regional solidarity. They also argued that Cameroon would lose important customs duties through the agreement.

There was no real change in Cameroon's relationships with Western countries, the major providers of debt relief and development aid. These remained fairly good despite President Biya's failure to engage in national or democratic dialogue before the constitutional change of April, as suggested by France and the US. *France*, which remained Cameroon's main trading partner and source of private investment and foreign aid, decided in October to resume its loans to Yaoundé. These had been suspended in 2001 at the beginning of the debt cancellation process. Prior to this announcement, the Biya regime had strengthened its relations with Paris with the visit in May by the French minister of immigration, national identity and development, Brice Hortefeux, long-time friend and close ally of President Sarkozy. He held talks in Yaoundé with President Biya, who had met with the French president in October 2007 in Paris.

Relationships between Cameroon and the *US* were more strained. The US administration decided to apply Proclamation 7750 issued at the January 2004 Summit of the Americas in Monterrey, Mexico, to Cameroonian citizens. This document stiffened US immigration laws by mandating the denial of visas to "persons engaged in or benefiting from egregious official corruption." Its extension to Cameroonians was decided "because official words and declarations have had little effect", according to a diplomat at the US embassy.

In September, President Biya attended the UN General Assembly in New York and the Francophonie Summit in Canada in October. What caught the Cameroonian media's attention about these occasions was that the head of state spent 45 days abroad instead of caring about the country's increasingly difficult situation.

On 26 October, Pope Benedict XVI declared he would visit Yaoundé in March 2009 to attend the meeting of the Episcopal Conference of Africa. The last papal visit to Cameroon had been by John Paul II in 1995.

Socioeconomic Developments

The *2008 budget* was not very different from the previous one and stood at CFAfr 2,276 bn, an increase of 1.1% compared to 2007. Oil revenues were estimated to decrease from CFAfr 688 bn to CFAfr 593 bn. Despite policy changes by the government after the February riots, prices for commodities continued to increase throughout the year. Because of higher inflation (5.3% versus 1.1% in 2007), the 15% increase in salaries for civil servants had no major impact on consumers.

Government expenditures had to be increased as a consequence of the price hikes. The IMF showed understanding for those measures and extended its PRGF arrangement by half a year to January 2009. The IMF continued to admonish the government to increase domestic fuel prices in line with international oil prices. Fuel subsidies to consumers had already cost the national budget CFAfr 144 bn by midyear.

By the end of the year, the government owed CFAfr 142 bn to the national oil refinery SONARA. The business community expressed concern that the government could amass more domestic arrears, with a negative effect on already weak business confidence.

After the riots in February, a major emergency programme to boost agricultural production was announced in April, but by the end of the year farmers said they had seen no evidence of this plan on the ground. In October, the government also announced that family agriculture would benefit from a three-year plan worth CFAfr 30 bn, thanks to the contract on debt relief and development (C2D) signed with France. Meanwhile, ACDIC reported in December that the maize crop, the main cereal consumed by Cameroonians, would not be sufficient in 2009 and warned of a shortfall of about 120,000 tonnes if nothing more was done to help farmers.

Private companies continued to complain of *fiscal harassment and corruption*. For 2008, the World Bank ranked Cameroon 164 out of 181 in terms of ease of doing business (152 out of 175 in 2007). In December, less than a quarter of state-owned companies had submitted financial statements for 2007, according to the 'Chambre des Comptes de la Cour Supreme', which has been in charge of auditing finances since 2006. Moreover, it reported that audited financial statements contained many irregularities. According to an international expert, Dutch Professor Michel van Hulten, who worked for the national anti-corruption programme Change Habits, Oppose Corruption (CHOC) launched by the main donors to the country and the government, "the so-called 'political will' to fight corruption in reality does not exist."

The employers' federation 'Groupement Interpatronal du Cameroun' (Gicam) reported in October that the *illegal trade* in fuel between Nigeria and Cameroon was causing monthly losses of CFAfr 13 bn to the companies involved in fuel distribution. The report continued that the state was also losing several CFAfr billions of taxes and custom duties. Gicam underlined that some authorities were involved in the illegal traffic.

Gicam also complained at the end of the year of the continuing lack of sound *transportation infrastructure* in the economic capital, Douala. The employers especially stressed the too-slow rehabilitation work on the only bridge connecting the city to the industrial area of Bonabéri. Some companies reported that the huge traffic jams caused by the work resulted in a 15% decrease in turnover.

Cameroon's *timber industry*, the second most important export sector in the country, suffered heavily as a consequence of the global financial crisis. The sector began to be affected in March. About 10% of orders by American, Asian and European clients were cancelled. By the end of the year, 800 people had been laid off and the major firms in the sector announced that a further 2,000 people would be dismissed in January 2009 because of lack of demand. *Energy shortages* continued to handicap private companies. No tangible progress was made during the year on major dam projects such as the Lom Pangar dam, which should substantially improve the power supply. Mining exploitation did not progress either. The ministry of mining noted, nevertheless, that 53 exploration permits were registered during the year, as against only two in 2003. For instance, Nu Energy Corporation Cameroon, part of the Canadian Mega Uranium company, began exploring for uranium at two sites in the north and south of the country.

The only major *investment* of the year was in the cement industry, a strategic sector, since Cameroon supplies several countries of the sub-region. The main player, Cimencam, owned by the French company Lafarge and the state of Cameroon, invested CFAfr 26 bn in a new crusher that will increase cement production from 900,000 tonnes to 1.5 m tonnes. The government expects this investment to bring an end to the chronic shortage of cement.

After a failed attempt at privatisation, the international carrier, *Cameroon Airlines* (Camair), placed in liquidation in 2005, discontinued its activities in March and was dissolved in May, at which time its 800 employees were dismissed. Camairco, the company created by President Biya in September 2006 to replace Camair, has still to be established. The company's demise was seen as a crucial problem, since Camair had been the main transportation link connecting the northern and southern parts of the country.

Cameroon in 2009

Throughout the year in Cameroon, there was an awareness of the 2011 presidential election being on the horizon. President Biya and his party, which continued to dominate the political scene, seemed to be already preparing for election day, as public criticism emerged for the first time about the president's wealth. As a consequence of the global financial crisis, the economy tended to slow down, with a sharp drop in oil revenues. No major social unrest was recorded.

Domestic Politics

In January, the main opposition party, the Social Democratic Front (SDF), demanded the revision of the membership of *Elections Cameroon (ELECAM)*, the new institution created by law in 2006, whose responsibility is to organise and supervise elections, although all its members were from the ruling 'Rassemblement Démocratique du Peuple Camerounais' (RDPC). A few weeks later, the (EU) expressed regret that "most of the members" of ELECAM, named at the end of 2008 by Biya, belonged to the ruling party. The authorities did not react to this publicly, but in an address to the members of the diplomatic community gathered in his ministry, the minister of external relations, Henri Eyebe Eyebe Ayissi, admonished them to respect Cameroon's sovereignty and asked them to refrain from making comments that would discredit ELECAM. The last six months of the year were marked by a strong *mobilisation of the RDPC* and its chairman, President Paul Biya, apparently already on the starting-blocks for the 2011 presidential election. As with the 25th anniversary celebrations of the Biya regime (2007) and the change in the Constitution (2008), mobilisation started with a large increase in the notorious 'motions of support' for the head of state, asking for his candidacy in 2011, and these were reported daily by the public media. The RDPC, though weakened by factional divisions, also organised numerous meetings throughout the country as if the electoral campaign had already begun. Some party members insisted that the poll should be brought forward from 2011 to 2010. In November, on the occasion of the 27th anniversary of his accession to power, 76 year-old Biya thanked his supporters for their 'calls' in an open letter, but remained elusive about his plans, not stating clearly whether he would run for the presidency. However, he implied that he wanted to stay in power by asserting to the Cameroon people that he would "go the whole way to find solutions to the painful problem of unemployment of young people" and to improve moral standards and fight against corruption and the embezzlement of public funds.

A few months before, the RDPC had been on the defensive because of a heated argument that directly affected Biya. For the first time, the national media discussed his wealth and his use of public funds. The controversy was first caused by a report written in June by the French NGO 'Comité Catholique Contre la Faim' about the "dishonestly acquired property" of several African heads of state, including Biya. The RDPC strongly defended its chairman, but the debate was reactivated in August with articles in the French media about the cost of *Biya's vacation in France*. According to these reports, the president had stayed for three weeks in August at the coastal resort of La Baule, with a delegation of 40 people, occupying 43 rooms in two prestigious hotels at a cost of about € 900,000. The government and the RDPC denounced the reports as a "media conspiracy". The opposition parties, who were largely absent from the political scene throughout the year, took the opportunity to react. John Fru Ndi, chairman of the SDF, said Biya's stay in La Baule would amount to a true scandal, adding, "Since his accession in power in 1982, Paul Biya and his acolytes are only ransacking the Cameroonian people." Bernard Muna, Chairman of the 'Alliance des Forces du Progrès', an SDF splinter party, was equally outspoken and criticised the president's behaviour in the middle of an economic crisis.

A *cabinet reshuffle* took place on 30 June: Biya sacked Prime Minister Ephraïm Inoni, who had been appointed in 2004. Philemon Yang, 62, a magistrate from the Anglophone North West region who had been minister and deputy secretary general at the Presidency, was appointed as his successor. Inoni, a native of the South West region, was dismissed, as his name had often been mentioned in connection with corruption during recent years. Equally significant was the removal of Defence Minister Rémy Ze Meka. He was replaced by the chief of police, Edgar Alain Mebe Ngo'o, a long-time ally of President Biya. Seven other ministers also lost their jobs.

The *February 2008 riots* were still a matter of controversy. In February, the 'Observatoire National des Droits de l'Homme du Cameroun' (ONDH), a federation of human rights NGOs, deplored the absence of an official inquiry into responsibility for the violence and condemned the excessive use of force by the army and the police, accusing them of serious human rights violations. The ONDH also maintained that at least 139 people had been killed. The government replied that the final death toll was 40 and that the ONDH's figures were "not true and not credible". In January, the mayor of Njombé-Penja (South) and member of the ruling party, Paul Eric Kingué, was sentenced to six years' imprisonment for his alleged participation in the riots in his city against a French-owned banana plantation, the Plantations du Haut Penja (PHP). He was also condemned with 17 others to pay the company € 1.2 m in damages. Some NGOs said his condemnation was related to his ambition to break up a corruption network involving the PHP and another French-owned banana plantation company in his home area. In June, the singer Lapiro de Mbanga, very famous in the early 1990s, was sentenced on appeal to three years' imprisonment. He had been arrested in April 2008 and subsequently charged with looting during the riots.

Corruption remained an important topic of public debate. An old case returned to the political scene in October, when a new trial for corruption was launched against Titus Edzoa, already condemned

in 1999. Former secretary general at the Presidency and formerly
Biya's personal physician for many years, Edzoa was sentenced in
1999 to 15 years in prison for embezzlement. He had been arrested
in 1997, a few days after his resignation as health minister and his
announcement to stand as a candidate in the 1997 presidential election. In the new case, Edzoa and his co-accused, including a former
minister in the president's office, were charged with embezzling a
total of CFAfr 61 bn (€ 91 m). Edzoa claimed that he was the victim
of a "political conspiracy".

The government's *anti-corruption campaign* 'Epervier' seemed to
slow down, compared with spectacular arrests carried out in the previous year. In August, the former head of the state-owned petroleum
distribution company 'Société Camerounaise des Dépôts Pétroliers'
(SCDP), Jean Baptiste Nguini Effa, and six of his aides were arrested, all suspected of having embezzled public funds. A few months
before, Nguini Effa had been ordered to repay € 1.4 m and to pay a
fine of € 3,000 for misappropriating funds while managing SCDP. In
July, seven finance officers and cashiers employed by the city government in Douala were arrested on charges of embezzling € 3 m.
Former energy minister Alphonse Siyam Siwé, initially condemned
to 30 years in prison in 2007, was sentenced to life on appeal in June
for the embezzlement with 12 other people of € 53 m when he was
head of the 'Port Autonome de Douala'. A former high official at the
health ministry, arrested in 2006, was sentenced in July to 15 years in
prison for having embezzled funds provided by donor organisations
to fight the spread of HIV/AIDS. Former ministers Polycarpe Abah
Abah, Urbain Olanguena Awono and Jean-Marie Atangana Mebara,
who were arrested in 2008, were still awaiting trial.

Despite these actions, critics questioned the will of the authorities
to seriously fight corruption. The case of the *'Association Citoyenne
de Défense des Intérêts Collectifs'* (ACDIC) raised most attention in
the media. In May, Bernard Njonga, chairman of ACDIC, was given
a suspended two-month sentence for "illegal demonstration". He
was accused of having held a meeting at the ACDIC headquarters in

Yaoundé in December 2008, to protest against the embezzlement of funds at the ministry of agriculture. According to an ACDIC report, 62% of a € 1.8 m grant to support the production of maize had been misappropriated in 2008 by civil servants in the ministry. Faced with the strong mediatisation of this affair, the head of the 'Commission Nationale de Lutte contre la Corruption' (CONAC), a state body mostly inactive since its creation in 2006, had launched an inquiry into the embezzlements. Its report confirmed the ACDIC data and highlighted the culpability of 47 individuals, most of them employees at the ministry, but the CONAC document was never published. In September, ACDIC decided to lodge a complaint against the 47 employees to avoid the affair being entirely forgotten.

Domestic *insecurity* remained a matter of concern. Pirate attacks at sea were numerous off the Bakassi peninsula. In March, four employees of Tidewater, a multinational firm that provides maritime services to the oil industry, were kidnapped off the Bakassi peninsula. They were freed in July. According to the Cameroonian media, a large ransom was paid to the kidnappers. No public information was given by the authorities, who even denied the incident had taken place. In the same period, three Filipino fishermen and two Ukrainian mechanics were seized from a trawler off the Cameroon coast and were later released, apparently without a ransom being paid to their captors. The abduction was initially blamed on the Nigerian guerilla group Movement for the Emancipation of the Niger Delta, but this group, active in Nigeria's oil-rich south, denied any involvement. In October, the new defence minister, Edgar Alain Mebe Ngo'o, said that Cameroonian troops had killed four armed pirates who had attacked a private boat off Bakassi, and one person was killed in a different attack on a trawler. In late December, a policeman was killed by pirates in an assault on a boat. Some media reports said that responsibility for the attack was claimed by the Bakassi Freedom Fighters, a small armed group from the peninsula, who had kidnapped nine French oil company workers in 2008. At the end of the year, attacks by bandits were also frequent

in the Northern regions. In November, seven people were killed by
bandits armed with automatic weapons in less than a week. Several
jailbreaks took place during the year, proving that *prison conditions*
remained poor and worrying. In June, 51 prisoners escaped from
the prison in Yagoua (Far North), and only 33 of them were recap-
tured. In July, 17 prisoners escaped from the prison in Meri (North).
In October, two prisoners were shot dead and two others wounded
during an attempted jailbreak at Bafoussam (West). A report by the
'Commission Nationale des Droits de l'Homme', an official body,
denounced the delays in the justice system. Preventive detention,
i.e. imprisonment before trial, accounts for 62% of all those held in
Cameroonian prisons and can last up to nine years. Conditions in
detention were "draconian, inhuman, degrading", it added. A report
published in January by Amnesty International (AI) caused quite a
stir: The report, 'Impunity underpins persistent abuse', registered
numerous human rights violations "approved or committed" by the
authorities and whose perpetrators escaped with "almost total impunity". AI complained that its inquiry teams had not been permit-
ted to visit Cameroon for 10 years.

Two *journalists* were sentenced during the year. The first was
Lewis Medjo, the publisher of the weekly 'La Détente Libre', who
has been imprisoned in the southwestern city of Douala since
26 September 2008 for publishing a report about an alleged ploy
by President Biya to force the President of the Supreme Court to
retire early. A court sentenced him on 7 January to three years in
prison and a fine of CFAfr 2 m on a charge of disseminating false
news. In December, Jean Bosco Talla, managing editor of the weekly
'Germinal', was sentenced to a one-year suspended term and a fine
of CFAfr 3.15 m for insulting the head of state. Talla had been arrested and jailed a few days after publishing passages from a book
alleging that, before becoming president, Biya pledged fidelity to his
predecessor, Ahmadou Ahidjo, in a secret pact that was sealed by "a
homosexual act". The French NGO 'Reporters Sans Frontières' urged
the Cameroonian authorities to de-criminalise press offences. This

position was shared by associations of Cameroonian journalists who, at the same time, pointed to the lack of a sense of responsibility among many of their colleagues. At the end of the year, the employees of 'Le Messager', the country's oldest private daily newspaper, went on strike to demand their salaries, which had not been paid for seven months. The chairman of the 'Syndicat National des Journalistes Employés du Cameroun', Norbass Tchana Ngante, stated that there were constant problems with the payment of salaries in all the private media and questioned their directors' probity.

In November, Cardinal Christian Tumi, archbishop of Douala, retired. He was well-known for his constant critical stance against the Biya regime, and for speaking out against corruption and the lack of justice and democracy. In contrast, during the three-day visit of Pope *Benedict XVI* in March, Biya and his wife attended popular masses celebrated in the Yaoundé stadium and in the historical Mvolyé basilica, and the Pope avoided addressing any of Tumi's major concerns with Cameroonian politics. This disappointed many Catholic believers, but confirmed the support of the majority of the local Catholic hierarchy.

Foreign Affairs

The government continued working to strengthen the special relationship with *France*, which remained Cameroon's principle trading partner and a main source of private investment and foreign aid. On 24 July, President Biya met President Nicolas Sarkozy at the Elysée during a state visit to Paris. A few weeks before, French Prime Minister François Fillon paid an official visit to Yaoundé and was received by Biya. Both signed a new defence partnership agreement, putting an end to a set of partially secret agreements concluded in 1974, which had provided for automatic French military assistance if Cameroon was attacked. Fillon also signed a bilateral migration agreement regulating the access of Cameroonian migrants to the

French labour market. In March, the French secretary of state for cooperation, Alain Joyandet, also came to Cameroon and made a notable visit to the French-owned banana plantation PHP in Njombé-Penja.

Biya attended the funeral of *Gabon*'s President Omar Bongo Ondimba in Libreville in June. The government followed closely the presidential election in Gabon on 30 August, but did not side with any of the candidates. Former interior minister André Mba Obame, who officially came third in the elections, spent three weeks as a refugee in the Cameroonian embassy in Libreville immediately after the poll, claiming that he feared for his life. The first official visit made by the newly elected president, Ali Bongo Ondimba, son of Omar, was to Cameroon, on 11 September. He was welcomed with full honours at the airport by Biya himself. Relations between the two countries had been characterised by fierce competition over the past decades.

At the end of his mandate in December, the EU representative in Yaoundé, Javier Pujol, criticised the government's fight against corruption. In particular, he deplored the fact that the constitutional requirement for a declaration of property by ministers and members of parliament had not been implemented. He complained about the lack of desire for reform and criticised the excessive number of ministers (about 60). Pujol also expressed his doubts as to the credibility and neutrality of the members of ELECAM. This was a rare show of outspokenness within the diplomatic corps.

No ceremony was held in August to mark the first anniversary of the official handing over of the Bakassi peninsula to Cameroon by *Nigeria* on 14 August 2008, in line with an international court ruling. In December, a first boundary stone was erected at Banki-Amchide in north Cameroon in the presence of Cameroonian and Nigerian officials, foreign diplomats and UN officials. About 1,950 km have to be marked. The EU said there were more than 3,000 boundary stones to be erected and that the EU had contributed € 4 m to the project. The *Chadian* President Idriss Deby Itno visited Biya in Yaoundé on

28–29 October. Deby thanked Biya for his support when Chad was attacked by rebels in May. Asserting that the relationship between the two countries was "excellent", they also spoke about insecurity in northern Cameroon, including attacks by bandits and kidnappings for ransom. Biya said he wanted a "permanent dialogue" on this matter.

The relationship with *Equatorial Guinea* remained strained. President Biya did not attend the swearing-in ceremony of President Teodoro Obiang Nguema in December, after his easy re-election. In January, the media reported that three Equato-Guinean soldiers had been arrested and detained for a few days on the southern border. One of them was accused of having killed a Cameroonian fisherman. According to the national media, he was kept in jail and the other two were freed. In May, about 300 Cameroonian illegal immigrants were expelled from Malabo to Douala. Four months later, 100 more illegal immigrants, including 71 Cameroonians, met the same fate.

Socioeconomic Developments

The 2009 *budget* stood at CFAfr 2,301 bn, an increase of 1.1% compared with 2008. Oil revenues were estimated to have decreased from CFAfr 593 bn to CFAfr 519 bn. About 59% of expenditure was devoted to government spending, 26% to investment and 15% to servicing debt. The government chose to renew the suspension of customs duties on several imported consumer goods. This measure was initially taken in response to the February 2008 riots. The global financial crisis had a clear impact on the Cameroonian economy. In his end-of-year speech, President Biya himself recognised that exports of wood, aluminium, cotton and rubber had fallen and the decline would be aggravated by the fall in prices of raw materials on the world market. The slow-down in economic activity would also result in a decline in tax and customs revenues and a loss of jobs. Some earmarked foreign investments were postponed. Oil revenues in particular decreased to a significant degree. Credit transfers to the public treasury from the state-owned 'Société Nationale des Hydrocarbures' (SNH) had fallen to CFAfr 331.76 bn from CFAfr 651.75 bn in 2008. Volumes of oil sold by the SNH had fallen to 17.624 m barrels against 20.231 m barrels in 2008. According to SNH, insecurity in the Bakassi area was also partly responsible. In April, the IMF warned that the growth of GDP would slow down because of the crisis and the fall in crude oil prices. It forecast a growth rate of 2.5% instead of 3.4% in 2008 and instead of 4% as projected by the 2009 budget. The IMF granted a loan of $ 144.1 m to help the country face the crisis in July. The World Bank signed two agreements worth $ 100 m in September for the development of agriculture and health, education, water, transport in rural areas.

In November, the government published a new *growth and employment strategy* paper ('Document de Stratégie pour la Croissance et l'Emploi'), replacing the PRSP adopted in 2003 and developed at international donors' request. The new plan is intended to help the country towards a GDP growth rate of 5.5% per year for the next 10 years. The government also expected to bring the rate of unemployment from more than 13% down to less than 7%. According to Prime Minister Yang, PRSP had allowed positive growth rates but had not helped to reduce poverty substantially. The business climate in Cameroon was termed "noxious" by the *World Bank*. The country was ranked 173 out of 183 countries by the Bank's yearly 'Doing Business' report, falling four places compared with the previous year. A representative of the World Bank declared that government reforms would not encourage substantial investment, and asked for limitation on corruption, a better tax system and a more impartial justice system. In December, the World Bank found Cameroon's growth achievement disappointing. The country would not be on-track to meet most of the MDGs. The report associated the extremely high under-employment with risks of social unrest and instability. In this regard, the impact of a decade of fiscal austerity, poor governance and unequal distribution of public services was found to be particularly problematic. The World Bank also noted that there was one doctor per 583 people in Biya's home region (South) compared with one doctor per 20,662 in the North region and the report described around one-third of all children as chronically malnourished. The World Bank's vice president for Africa, Obigieli Ezekwesili, said that, thanks to its debt reduction, Cameroon should be able to invest money in important sectors such as health, education and important economic infrastructure. "Unfortunately (...), what has happened is that Cameroon, unlike countries like Ghana which used the opportunity to generate strong growth of 5–6%, has the whole period been growing at levels of 2–3% on the average, which is well below expectations," she said.

Energy supply continued to be a matter of concern throughout the year. Although Cameroon was still planning to spend CFAfr 6 bn to increase electricity output from 1,000 MW to 3,000 MW by 2020, no real progress was observed in 2009, apart from the start-up of a new thermal power station (86 MW) in Yassa-Dibamba, close to Douala. The construction schedule for the Lom Pangar dam, which was supposed to supply more than half of the planned increase in capacity, was also still unclear. In May, about 20 organisations protested against the increase in power cuts. The assessment of the privatisation of the 'Société Nationale d'Electricité' would be calamitous, the NGOs said, asking for an end to the private monopoly on the public power service. In 2001, the government granted this monopoly to an American group, AES Sirocco, which held 51% of the capital of the company, the rest being held by the State (44%) and employees (5%).

Serious problems also emerged with the *railway company* Camrail, a concession of the French group Bolloré Africa Logistics: in August, a train carrying 1,000 people from Ngaoundéré (Adamaoua) was derailed in Yaoundé. Five people were killed and 303 injured. A few days later, another train carrying oil products from Douala was also derailed in Yaoundé and caught fire. One person died.

Some strategic decisions were taken in the *oil sector*. In December, Cameroon's state-owned oil refinery, the 'Société Nationale de Raffinage' (SONARA) signed a CFAfr 45 bn loan agreement with the Cameroon-based private Afriland First Bank, which also has branches in Equatorial Guinea, Democratic Republic of the Congo and São Tomé and Príncipe. This loan was intended to be used to raise the production capacity of SONARA from 2.1 to 3.5 m tonnes a year. The project should also enable the refinery to process the heavy crude that Cameroon produces. SONARA, which has been operational since 1981, has so far only refined light crude oil imported from Angola, Equatorial Guinea and Nigeria. Cameroon signed four new contracts with oil companies. In April, China's Yan Chang Logone Development Holding Company Ltd signed a $ 62 m production sharing contract for oil exploration on two onshore blocks in northern Cameroon. In July, Cameroon gave the French oil group Total-E&P (which already controlled about 65% of the country's oil production) the right to explore an off shore block in the Rio del Rey basin (South West), off the Bakassi peninsula. The Swiss firm Glencore was also given a permit to carry out offshore explorations in the same area. Noble Energy Inc. and Petronas Carigali Gas Ltd jointly won a contract to explore and drill for oil in the Campo basin (South). The two firms are already partners in Cameroon oil investment, and Petronas is a shareholder in the Chad-Cameroon Pipeline.

Some new trends became evident in the *mining sector*. In September, Australia's Legend Mining Ltd acquired a 90% interest in two permits for iron ore exploration in Ngovayang (South) and Mayo Binka (North). In October, Cameroon Alumina Ltd (a joint venture set up in 2008 by Dubai Aluminium Company Ltd and India's Hindalco Industries, along with US firm Hydromine Inc.) announced having found 550 m tonnes of bauxite deposits at their Ngaoundal and Minim-Martap properties (North). According to the company, the site could produce 4.5 to 9 m tonnes of bauxite per year starting in late 2014. Cameroon Alumina Ltd was projected to build an aluminium refinery with a capacity of 1.4 to 3 m tonnes and was discussing with the authorities the upgrading and extending of existing railway links from the mines to the Kribi deep-sea port. Australia's Sundance Resources, which has a permit for iron ore exploration in Mbalam, announced a two-year delay in starting production at the $ 2.46 bn project (i.e. until 2013). Once operational, Sundance hopes to produce some 35 m tonnes of ore per year. Geovic, which expects to produce 4,200 tonnes of cobalt per year and 2,100 tonnes of nickel per year for 21 years in Nkamouna (East), also said in early 2009 that, because of the global financial crisis, production would be delayed until 2012 and that investment had been cut to $ 250 m from $ 370 m. As in 2008, the government did not publish any reports on the framework of the Extractive Industries Transparency Initiative.

Cameroon in 2010

As in the previous year, the 2011 presidential election was the central concern for all political actors. As if already campaigning, President Paul Biya, who does not usually travel inside the country except to his home village, made an official visit to the capital of the sensitive North-West region. There, he met for the first time his longstanding rival, John Fru Ndi, chairman of the main opposition party, which was still challenging the administration of the election. During the year, the regime had to face several scandals, including one caused by the death in custody of a journalist. The economy was depressed, major infrastructure development projects continued to be stalled and oil production continued to decline.

Domestic politics

President Biya continued to maintain uncertainty over whether he would stand again as a candidate in the 2011 *presidential election*. However, two events suggested that he would: Biya, who rarely attends meetings with his peers, tried to gain international recognition by organising in May in Yaoundé a "high level" conference named 'Africa 21' to celebrate the 50th anniversary of the Independence of African former French colonies. Only three African presidents, Ali Bongo (Gabon), Blaise Compaoré (Burkina Faso) and Fradique de Menezes (São Tomé), and some international figures, such as former UN Secretary-General Kofi Annan, Chairman of the African Union Commission Jean Ping, and a number of French political leaders, including Secretary of State for Cooperation Alain Joyandet, Alain Juppé (mayor of Bordeaux) and Michel Rocard, attended the event. A similar motive was suspected for the official visit that Biya made in December to Bamenda, capital of the North-West region, where celebrations for the 50th anniversary of the Cameroonian army were the pretext for a meeting with his long-term rival, John Fru Ndi, chairman of the main opposition party, the Social Democratic Front (SDF). Biya does not usually travel inside the country and his last visit to Bamenda, stronghold of the SDF, was in 1991. Furthermore, Biya had previously always refused official meetings with Fru Ndi, who continued to claim victory at the 1992 presidential elections. The ruling Cameroon People's Democratic Movement (CPDM) publicised the Biya-Fru Ndi meeting through the media, repeating its slogan of "appeased democracy", but many citizens did not seem to appreciate seeing Fru Ndi, whose credibility was already very low, shaking hands with Biya and some accused the SDF chairman of playing the president's game. Moreover, Fru Ndi, like Biya, did not say whether he would run in the presidential election.

Before this event, the SDF, along with other parties and civil society organisations, continually criticised *Elections Cameroon* (ELECAM), the electoral body. In particular, they protested in March, when the CDPM pushed through an amendment increasing the involvement of the government in the organisation and conduct of the elections and making consultation with civil society optional. They all called for the dissolution of ELECAM, but refrained from extensive campaigning. In late August, the SDF published a list of 11 requirements for the presidential election, threatening to prevent the holding of the 2011 ballot if these requirements, including the appointment of new members of ELECAM and the withdrawal of the government from the electoral process, were not met. The regime did not react. In October, the SDF made a new attempt: in a complaint to the Supreme Court, the party demanded the cancellation of the voter registration process, which had started in August, claiming that ELECAM had been illegitimately established. The text of the law required that the instatement of ELECAM should be by presidential decree, which apparently had been omitted. A few days later, Biya signed the missing decree without comment. The SDF also reacted through a statement by its Douala MP, Jean Michel Nintcheu, to the publishing in April of the results of the census held in 2005: according to Nintcheu, the regime had inflated figures for some regions and reduced them for others, to its own electoral advantage. According to projections based on the 2005 census, Cameroon had in January 2010 19,406,100 citizens (compared with 10.5 m in 1987, according to the previous census).

As in 2009, the government had to face several scandals, some of them involving severe *human rights violations*. In April, the death in prison of a journalist, Germain Cyrille Ngota Ngota, gave rise to numerous criticisms, both within and outside the country. Ngota, managing editor of a small newspaper, was detained in April with two other journalists. All three were charged with having forged the signature of the president's chief of staff, Laurent Esso. Ngota's family said he suffered from high blood pressure and a hernia that needed surgery and alleged that he did not receive proper treatment in custody, while the government attributed his death to HIV infection and related diseases. This statement increased the controversy, as the Cameroonian medical association criticised the government for breaching medical confidentiality. In May, on international freedom of the press day, about 300 journalists tried to demonstrate peacefully in Yaoundé, asking for details about Ngota's death and calling for media offences to be decriminalised. The demonstration was brutally put down by the security forces. The two journalists who were jailed with Ngota were only released in November. In December, the International Federation of Journalists (IFJ) issued a statement expressing its deep concern about the deteriorating security situation for journalists in Cameroon, mentioning Ngota's death as well as "violent acts perpetrated by members of the security forces" against journalists. According to the IFJ, a few days before, on 10 December, a journalist with the private daily newspaper 'Le Jour' had been arrested in Ngaoundéré (North) without a written arrest warrant and threatened with death for having reported incidents involving Cameroonian army officers.

In addition to the Ngota scandal, the general governance of the regime was called into question several times, notably by some foreign organisations, which put the government on the defensive and forced it to respond publicly. Thus, in July it strongly criticised two reports published by the ICG, which described the risk that the country could fall into crisis, notably due to disputes within the regime, and pointed to the constitutional uncertainty that would surround the presidential inter-regnum should Biya be declared incapacitated: the amended constitution adopted in 1996 stipulates that the president of the Senate should take over if the president is incapacitated or dies in office, but that institution had yet to be created.

In November, a preliminary inquiry was opened by the Paris public prosecutor's office after a *complaint against Biya* lodged by the 'Union pour une diaspora active' for "concealment or misappropriation of public funds". President Biya, having "no assets in France or elsewhere ... does not feel at all concerned by these denunciations," said a press release from the presidency without further comment, as the CDPM and the government made numerous statements to defend the president. A large proportion of Cameroonians did not believe the regime's assertions.

The government also had several *security problems*, which revealed major flaws within the system: in early July, the national television headquarters in Yaoundé was the target of an attempted attack by unidentified armed men who were repelled by police. In the same period, a rumour of a coup attempt was widely covered in the press. According to the media, a group of alleged coup plotters wanted to seize power during Biya's stay in Paris for the French national day celebrations on 14 July. At the beginning of September, Biya sacked the police chief and the head of internal security. He named 78-year-old Martin Mbarga Nguele as the new police chief to replace Emmanuel Edou, who had been promoted to the position only in July 2009. Leopold Maxime Eko Eko was appointed head of the 'Direction Générale de la Recherche Extérieure' (DGRE), an intelligence agency, replacing previous chief Jean Marie Obelabout. No reason was given for the changes, but newspapers speculated that the president was beefing up his security after the rumoured July plot against him. Obelabout's role in the arrest of journalist Bibi Ngota, who was allegedly tortured at DGRE headquarters, probably contributed to his dismissal.

In late November, the commander of the 'Bataillon d'Intervention Rapide' (BIR), the Israeli former military officer Avraham Sivan, who was also in charge of security for Biya, was killed with three others in a military helicopter crash between Douala and Yaoundé. Formerly defence attaché at the Israeli Embassy in Yaoundé, Sivan was linked to the Cameroonian presidency by a private contract. He was also the military equipment and weapons provider for the BIR and the presidential guard.

Attacks at sea, including hostage-taking, proliferated during the year, particularly off the Bakassi Peninsula but also in areas close to the port of Douala, the economic capital. This raised concerns that the government was no longer able to protect even core parts of the country's territory. In March, a new armed group, the Africa Marine Commando (AMC), an off-shoot of the Bakassi Freedom Fighters (BFF), which had kidnapped ten oil sector workers in late 2008, abducted seven Chinese sailors from aboard two fishing boats off Bakassi. Reportedly held for a ransom of $ 15,000, the sailors were freed by Cameroonian security forces five days after their capture, according to the Cameroonian authorities. In the same period, two sailors, one Ghanaian and one Cameroonian, were also kidnapped and released a few days later. In May, two Russian sailors and a Lithuanian captain were taken hostage by pirates who attacked their ships, in the anchorage area of the port of Douala. They were released in Nigeria in early July following payment of ransoms. In September, the AMC also kidnapped six people – a Croatian, a Filipino and four Ukrainians – during an attack on three vessels moored off the port city of Douala. They were released about two weeks later. Cameroonian officials said they were freed in Cameroonian territory by its troops, but another source said they were freed by Nigerian forces in Nigeria. The AMC seemed to have taken hostages in order to call for the release of some of its fighters, who had been arrested and detained in the Buea prison (South-West).

In November, six people, including three members of the BIR, two Cameroonian civilians and one of the attackers, were killed in an attack on the oil platform Perenco off the Bakassi Peninsula for which the AMC claimed responsibility. In late March, a gendarmerie brigade in Bakassi Peninsula (South-West) was also attacked by an unidentified group, who took weapons but did not cause any casualties.

Foreign Affairs

On 14 July, Biya attended in Paris, *France*, the grandiose parade marking half a century of independence from colonial rule for former French colonies in Africa. Cameroonian soldiers in red uniforms were among those who paraded in the Avenue des Champs Elysees on Bastille Day. In Cameroon, this event and the national celebrations for the 50th anniversary of Independence were the opportunity for Cameroonian intellectuals and opposition members to express their anti-French sentiments. In April, several political parties, including the 'Mouvement Africain pour la Nouvelle Indépendance et la Démocratie' (MANIDEM) and the Mack-Kit wing of the historical opposition party the 'Union des Populations du Cameroun', trade unions and associations expressed their indignation, speaking of the provocation and paternalism of the French authorities' initiative and financial aid to commemorate the anniversary. They denounced 'Françafrique', referring to a perceived tradition of shady official and business ties between France and its former colonies, including Cameroon, implying that the latter was still under France's control.

During the year, Cameroon had two visitors from the UN: the Secretary-General Ban Ki-moon in June and the High Commissioner for Refugees Antonio Guterres in March. During his visit, Guterres revealed that, between 2008 and 2009 nearly 18,000 refugees from the CAR had fled their country for Cameroon, where their number exceeded 80,000. They were spread over 73 sites in the East and Adamawa regions, according to Guterres, who was received by Biya and visited two refugee camps in Eastern region. In June, Ban Ki-moon also met with Biya, who called for the allocation to Africa of at least one permanent place on the UNSC, reiterating a call he had already made in May at 'Africa 21'. Ban Ki-moon delivered a speech to the parliament, promising the "full support" of the UN to secure the Bakassi Peninsula.

In October, Cameroon and the EU signed a voluntary partnership agreement aimed at banning trade in illegally logged timber (Cameroon is Africa's largest exporter of timber to Europe), stipulating that by July 2012 all supplies of timber from Cameroon to the EU would be certified as legally sourced.

At the end of February, a new crisis in bilateral relations with the Equato-Guinean government erupted: Malabo accused troops from Cameroon of attacking a ship supplying an oil platform in Equatorial Guinea, allegedly because they wanted to steal the vessel. *Equatorial Guinea* asserted that the attackers were rogue soldiers belonging to the BIR. No deaths were reported, according to the Equatorial Guinean authorities, who said their radar had followed the vessel and that the "assailants" had fled, knowing they had been spotted. In response, Cameroon denied the alleged assault, claiming that it had arisen from the erroneous interpretation of a common and innocuous incident during a mission at sea by BIR forces, who were "lost" due to "particularly unfavorable weather conditions" and found themselves accidentally beyond the maritime boundary in the territorial waters of Equatorial Guinea.

In December, the secretary general of the president's office, Laurent Esso, and the deputy director of the foreign affairs office at the Chinese ministry of defence, Major General Jia Xiaoning, signed an agreement for military assistance, including the donation of military equipment. In 2009, *China* had already made a donation to the

Cameroonian gendarmerie consisting of helmets, shields and batons and had donated about CFAfr 210 m to the 'Ecole Internationale des Forces de Sécurité' (EIFORCES), located near Yaoundé.

In March, the *Turkey*'s President Abdullah Gül came to Yaoundé for a two-day official visit, the first by a Turkish president to Cameroon. "Between Turkey whose economy is booming and Cameroon.... which wants to accelerate its development, there is the promise of full complementarity", Biya said in an interview with Gül. The latter said that Turkey wanted to develop relations with Africa on a just basis that was likely to serve the common interests of their peoples. In August, Biya made an official visit to Brazil, where the Cameroonian minister of foreign affairs had visited a few months before to sign a number of cooperation agreements, including some in the field of agriculture.

Socioeconomic Developments

The *economic situation* remained unsatisfactory: none of the major infrastructure development projects (such as hydroelectric dams and the deep water port at Kribi) that Biya had promised and that were to provide employment had been started. In addition, there was no improvement in living conditions for the majority of the population. In February, a report by the National Institute of Statistic said that the number of people living in poverty had increased from 6.2 m in 2001 to 7.1 m (39.9% of the population) in 2007. According to the report, the North, Far North, Adamaoua and East regions were those most affected by poverty. In addition, there was an extensive outbreak of *cholera* in May in northern areas. The epidemic was the most severe for ten years and was reported in October to have killed about 559 people after spreading to other regions. Minister of Health Mama Fouda revealed that, in the populous areas of Yaoundé and Douala, 100% of the well water was unfit for consumption because of fecal contamination.

During the first six months of the year, the two main cities, Yaoundé and Douala, faced a *serious shortage of drinking water*. Fire brigades and members of the security forces were requisitioned to provide people with free water. According to the water provider Camwater, the shortage was due to the fall in the level of the Nyong River after the dry season. Promising to solve the problem, the government said that it had put in place a CFAfr 400 m programme to restore water sector infrastructure, which had received no investment for 20 years, according to the minister in charge of water, Michael Tomdio.

The 2010 *budget* stood at CFAfr 2,570 bn. About 59.4% of the expenditure was devoted to government spending, about 26.3% to investment and 14.3% to servicing debt. This budget was based on an assumption of real GDP growth of 3.9%. The government expected to receive about € 620 m in revenue from oil compared with € 791 m in 2009. The budget also relied on donations and loans (amounting to nearly € 337 m). However, Biya decided in September to reduce the budget by 2% following consultations with the IMF. According to the IMF, the government's original expenditure plans could not be reconciled with the long list of unsettled payment obligations carried forward from 2009, as well as unrealistic revenue estimates, the recapitalisation of a major bank and the delay in issuing CFAfr 200 bn of bonds on the Douala Stock Exchange. The bonds were finally issued in December and raised only about € 305 m for the government. The authorities said that the money would finance some high-priority development projects, including the construction of the hydroelectric dam at Lom-Pangar (East), the deepwater port at Kribi and the Memve'ele dam on the Ntem River (South), as well as road and agricultural projects and the relocation of part of the Chad-Cameroon Pipeline from the site of the planned dam at Lom-Pangar.

The state increased its fuel *subsidies* from a monthly average of CFAfr 1.75 m in 2009 to over CFAfr 10 bn in 2010, thereby avoiding an increase of the fuel prices for consumers. It also decided to subsidise electricity prices in September and about CFAfr 11 bn were paid to electricity company AES-Sonel. This was seen as a measure to stop popular anger erupting as in 2008, when price hikes led to large-scale demonstrations. In November, the public sector trade union planned a peaceful demonstration in Yaoundé to ask for higher wages and the standardisation of the retirement age in the public sector, but nine of its members, including its president, were arrested. Seven of them were then charged with public order offences. In December, 15 leaders of NGOs were also arrested in Yaoundé as they were preparing a demonstration calling for 15% of the national budget to be devoted to the health sector in accordance with the Abuja Declaration, ratified in 2001 by Cameroon. The activists were finally released without charge.

In January, the *World Bank* signed two loan agreements with Cameroon. The first was for $ 150 m for the road infrastructure between Cameroon and the neighbouring CAR and Chad. The second was for $ 9.9 m to expand the geographic range and use of optical fibres in the sub-region. In June, Cameroon and Congo signed an agreement for the construction of a 504-km road linking the two countries between Sangmélima (South Cameroon) and Ouesso (North Congo), with Cameroon to spend € 307 m. The World Bank issued a statement in February underlining that Cameroon, which has an annual growth rate target of 5.5% over the next ten years, would not be able to reach this goal without the growth of small and medium enterprises and the mining sector, the ending of the structural shortage of electricity and the acceleration of reforms to improve the business climate, which was still deemed disastrous.

Oil production continued to decline, falling by about 12.6% to an average 63,900 b/d, according to official sources. Indeed, output during the fourth quarter of 2010 averaged only 62,700 b/d, yielding CFAfr 115.9 bn for the treasury, according to the state oil company 'Société Nationale des Hydrocarbures'. The decline was the result of the combined effects of natural depletion of the fields, the delapidation of production equipment, and the postponement of several development projects caused by the international financial crisis. The authorities predicted that output would fall further in 2011 to around 55,000 b/d, but could rebound in 2012 when new wells should go into production. In November, the French oil giant Total said that it would divest mature exploration-production activities in Cameroon, accounting for about 0.3% of its production, to independent French group Perenco. The deal related to oil fields at a mature stage of development or nearing the end of their lives, producing about 40,000 b/d and representing 8,000 b/d in terms of the oil accruing to Total. In April, an oil spill occurred off Kribi at the Chad-Cameroon pipeline terminal as a tanker was filling up. Several NGOs criticised COTCO, the company operating the pipeline, for not providing details about the incident, which was officially the second oil spill in Cameroon since the Chad-Cameroon pipeline was opened in 2003.

The most significant progress in the *mining sector*, considered by the government as the future main source of state revenues, took place at Mobilong, near the town of Yocadouma (East), where large diamond deposits were discovered. In December, the government finally approved a bid by a South Korean company, Cameroon and Korea Mining Company Incorporation (C&K Mining Inc.), to exploit the mine. C&K, which had first received an exploration permit in 2007, had a 65% stake in the mine, with the other 35% held by the Cameroon government. The C&K operating licence was the first to be granted by Cameroon for diamonds and was reportedly for a period of 25 years renewable for a period not exceeding ten years. The site covers an area of 236 km², according to Biya's decree, which did not detail the importance of the diamond deposit.

In terms of governance, the *anti-corruption campaign* continued timidly, but many prominent Cameroonians were involved. In June, Minister of Justice Amadou Ali revealed that 50 cases relating to corruption were being investigated. Despite these efforts, Cameroon – together with seven other countries – was ranked 146th out of 178 countries in the 2010 TI report. In January, several senior officials, including three former members of the government, were arrested: Haman Adama, former minister of basic education (2003–2009) and nine others, including the former chief executive of the 'Aéroports du Cameroun' Roger Ntongo Onguene (2003–2009), the former minister of budget Henry Engoulou (2004–2006) and the former secretary of state at the ministry of secondary education Catherine Abena (2004–2009). In February, a former government representative in Bamenda was arrested and charged with embezzlement of public funds. In September, a former head of state-owned Cameroon Airlines (2000–2003) and son of a prominent Cameroonian businessman, Yves-Michel Fotso, was arrested in Douala and transferred to Yaoundé's central prison for complicity in the embezzlement of funds in the 'Albatross affair', a case that takes its name from a presidential plane bought in suspicious circumstances in 2003. In October, the former head of the state-owned shipyard 'Chantier Naval et Industriel du Cameroun', Zacchaeus Forjindam, who was arrested in 2008, was sentenced to 12 years' imprisonment for embezzlement of public funds. The trial of former minister Polycarpe Abah Abah was opened in March, a few days after the trial began of his former colleague Urbain Olanguena Awono. Both had been arrested in 2008.

In September, Cameroon published its third report on transparency, regarding revenues generated by oil and mining for the 2006–2008 period, in the framework of the Extractive Industries Transparency Initiative (EITI). The first report had been released in 2006, and the second in 2007. According to the new report, 11 companies (five in oil, six mining), as well as most state services, did not submit their data to the private firm charged with preparing the report, while others provided data late or in insufficient detail. For the three years covered by the assessment, those oil companies that complied with requests for information said they paid about € 530 m to the state compared with the official figure of nearly € 533 m. For the same period (2006–2008), mining companies said they had paid about € 865,000 while the state said it had received € 639,000.

No clear explanation was given about these discrepancies, which may mean that there had been misappropriation of funds or/and bad governance. Indeed, some analysts believe that the EITI reports in Cameroon do not represent the reality of the situation, as the figures given by the companies and the government are not checked by an independent body.

In February, 40 civil society organisations launched a temporary and localised *campaign against the consumption of imported food*, including rice and milk. The campaign was to take place at a national forum on agriculture to be organised in November in Ebolowa (South), but after several delays, the event was finally postponed by the presidency to January 2011.

Cameroon in 2011

The presidential election was without doubt the most important event of the year, although it took place against a background of general indifference. Unsurprisingly, 78-year-old President Paul Biya, already one of Africa's longest serving presidents (29 years), was re-elected against competition from 22 other candidates (a record) for a further term of seven years, receiving 78% of the votes, according to official figures. The leader of the Social Democratic Front (SDF), John Fru Ndi, seen as Biya's main opponent, received only 10% of the votes, his lowest ever result. NGOs and opposition political parties reported widespread fraud and described the organisation of the polls as chaotic. Throughout the year social tension was high, and the authorities maintained a high security force presence in public spaces.

Domestic Politics

The 9 October vote was preceded by a long period of political and social tension. In June, *a football match* played in Yaoundé between the national teams of Cameroon and Senegal escalated into *riots* after the match ended in a draw, preventing Cameroon from qualifying for the 2012 African Cup of Nations. Supporters clashed with police for several hours, and local newspapers reported that between one and four people were killed during the violence, although there was no official confirmation. In July, five people were killed, including four by lynching, and dozens injured in clashes between residents and criminals in Douala.

Spectacular acts of violence were also reported. In March, a bank robbery perpetrated by heavily armed men took place in the district of Bonabéri in Douala. The gang controlled the area for two hours and killed five people before escaping by boat on the Wouri River

© KONINKLIJKE BRILL NV, LEIDEN, 2019 | DOI:10.1163/9789004401532_005

with their booty (CFA fr 200 m – about € 305,000). A few weeks later, several soldiers and a navy captain were arrested, suspected of involvement in the case, which reinforced the impression of a high degree of *criminality in the Cameroonian security forces.*

As in the past three years, violence continued on the *Bakassi* peninsula (bordering Nigeria). In February, three attacks were recorded in less than a week. On 6 February, 13 people, including a sub-prefect, were kidnapped. They were released for a ransom after ten days of captivity. On the night of 6–7 February, the police station in Mbonjo was attacked and, according to the government, two policemen were killed. These two attacks were the work of the Africa Marine Commando (AMC), the most active armed group in the Bakassi region. According to the private daily newspaper 'Le Jour', the AMC was demanding that the five oil companies operating in Bakassi each pay a monthly tax of Naira 6 m (around € 150,000). Following these attacks, Paul Biya returned urgently from Switzerland, where he makes extended private visits, and ordered the establishment of a crisis committee. Only a few days later, another attack occurred at Isangele (Bakassi): a soldier and a civilian were killed.

On the political level, tension was particularly high in early February, when several small *opposition parties* (including the 'Union des populations du Cameroun' and the 'Mouvement Africain pour la Nouvelle Indépendance et la Démocratie' – Manidem), and the SDF MP of Wouri (Douala) Jean Michel Nintcheu, announced that they would organise *demonstrations.* Their aim was to celebrate the 'martyrs' of the riots of February 2008 and also to ask Biya not to stand in the elections. The anxious authorities publicly threatened opponents with reprisals, and cut the Twitter service for several days. Although the popular mobilisation was almost zero, a consequence of the widespread disinterest in politics among Cameroonians, a large number of security forces were deployed in Douala to prevent the coalition of parties from holding a meeting, scheduled for 23 February. On that date, they arrested the organisers of the meeting and transported them to the outskirts of Douala, where they were released. Nintcheu was beaten by the police but not arrested. A correspondent of 'Agence France Presse' who covered the event was arrested and detained for nearly 48 hours. No other demonstrations were attempted after this event, seen by some observers and citizens as a way for the opposition to put pressure on the government to extort money from it in return for withdrawing its threat to cause disturbances. Nevertheless, the authorities, who seemed to be frightened by the revolutions in Arab countries, maintained their tight control of both opposition moves and the media during the following weeks.

Thus, in March 2011, the National Assembly adopted a bill authorising the president to have telephones tapped without making a request through parliament. During the same period, the number of soldiers in the 'Brigade d'Intervention Rapide' (a special unit of the army, directly linked to the presidency) was revised upwards with the recruitment of 3,000 new members. In April, the long-time opposition activist, Mboua Massok, was arrested on several occasions, and the first edition of an International Human Rights Film Festival, organised in Yaoundé by several associations and funded by the EU, was banned by the authorities: only a few hours before the first screening, the authorities sent the riot police authorised by a prefectural ban mentioning a threat to public order. At the end of April, the authorities also banned a private screening in Yaoundé of the documentary 'The Big Banana', which is very critical of the activities of the Franco-American company 'Plantations du Haut-Penja'.

There was also perceptible *tension inside the ruling party*, the Cameroon People's Democratic Movement (CDPM). In June, a controversy erupted, fueled by disgruntled, but anonymous members of the ruling party, about the Biya's eligibility to stand for election for another term,. The assertion was that the Constitution, revised in 2008, would not allow Biya to stand in another election, because his mandate began in 2004 under a constitutional clause that limited the number of presidential terms, and that he could not take advantage of rules introduced after that date.

At the beginning of September, the publication by *Wikileaks* of numerous cables issued by the US embassy in Yaoundé generated new tension within the ruling party. For several days, newspapers re-published parts of this material, describing interviews between several prominent officials and US diplomats. According to one of the cables, Minister of State for Territorial Administration Marafa Hamidou Yaya admitted that he had ambitions to become president after Biya's term ended. Another cable detailed the ethnic theory supported by Deputy Prime Minister and Minister of Justice Amadou Ali, in a discussion with the US Ambassador. According to the source, Ali said the struggle for Biya's succession should be viewed through ethnic and regional lenses. He explained that the foundation of Cameroon's stability would be the detente between Biya's Beti/Bulu ethnic group (in the south), and the populations of Cameroon's northern region. Ali claimed that the north would support Biya for as long as he wanted to be president, but would not accept a successor who was either another Beti/Bulu, or a member of the economically powerful Bamileke ethnic group (originating from the west). "Ali's analysis and his willingness to speak so frankly about such a sensitive topic reinforced our conviction that Cameroon's political elite is increasingly focused on jockeying for the post-Biya era," the cable concluded, reflecting the fear of most observers that the tribalisation of Biya's regime would one day degenerate into inter-communal violence.

In September, the *CPDM held an ordinary congress*, which should normally be held every five years and be the time to revise the membership of the central committee, although the last congress had been held in 1996. The meeting, eagerly expected for a long time by the party's 'reformers', had in recent years been repeatedly announced and then postponed. By holding it, Biya seemed to want to prove to his foreign partners – who discreetly criticised his long tenure of power – that he still had the support of the CDPM, which de facto controls elections. Internally, a lot of members were waiting for a rejuvenation of the party leaders, wondering whether the president would try to stop the clan war raging in his party and his entourage about his heritage. There was finally no surprise: Biya was re-elected unopposed as the head of the party, silencing the rumours that had suggested he might hand over to a successor. The changes introduced by Biya were insignificant: the number of members of the Central Committee, the party's governing body, was increased (from 250 to 350, much more than the party rules allowed), as was the political bureau (from 23 to 30). Some individuals who were positioning themselves as 'renovators' or 'reformers' were appointed by Biya to the Central Committee and thereby silenced.

Until the very end, Biya remained vague about the *election*: he fixed the election date at the last moment and left many guessing about his candidacy. The date of the election (9 October) was in fact only announced on 30 August and Biya registered his candidacy on 4 September, the closing day for submissions, without any prior public statement. His candidacy documents were submitted at Elecam (the office charged with organising elections) by party officials, almost through the back door and the incumbent candidate hardly campaigned, attending only three meetings (in Maroua, Douala, Kribi), all in the week before the election.

His challengers were unable, however, to take advantage of this low-key public campaigning. The *opposition was again strongly disorganised*: in addition to Biya, 22 candidates were approved by Elecam (out of 52 submissions), which was a record. John Fru Ndi, the president of the SDF, was also silent for a long time about his own intentions, and it was only on 3 September that he was officially selected by his party to be their presidential candidate. In August, Fru Ndi had called on Cameroonians to register as voters just days before the registration deadline, which was seen as an important change in his attitude: in September 2010, he had encouraged Cameroonians not to register as voters and had also threatened to prevent the elections. He was at that time protesting on behalf of *Elecam*, demanding reforms to guarantee it more independence. The government did indeed introduce reforms, but not in that direction: in April, a new amendment, passed in a special session of the Parliament, took away Elecam's right to announce the provisional election results, which became the prerogative of the Supreme Court, acting on behalf of the Constitutional Council (one of the key institutions foreseen in the current Constitution, but not yet created). This was probably the Cameroonian authorities' reaction to the post-election crisis in Côte d'Ivoire in late 2010, which resulted from a conflict between the Independent Electoral Commission and the Constitutional Council. Other changes, introduced a few weeks later, gave more power to the ministries of justice and territorial administration in the organisation of elections.

At the end of September, a few days before the presidential elections, a bizarre incident occurred in Douala: *gunmen* wearing military uniforms and holding placards saying "Biya must go" blockaded the bridge over the Wouri, shooting at police for some hours. There was no clear explanation of this episode. Many Cameroonians suspected that the authorities were behind it, creating a pretext to militarise the country before the election, and security measures were in fact greatly enhanced in the days following the incident.

The presidential election was held on 9 October without major incident, although the SDF claimed that, an SDF party worker was killed in the western region of Bandjoun by supporters of the ruling party, and a previously unknown armed group called the 'Commando Alliance Brotherhood of Cameroon' claimed responsibility for the killing of two soldiers at a polling station in Isangele. Even though the voting took place without major violence, it was marked by widespread voter apathy: observers and NGOs, including Transparency International Cameroon, estimated the real rate of participation at less than 30%, although the official figure was 65.8%. The organisation of the polls itself attracted much criticism from the opposition, observers and some foreign partners. The SDF spoke of a "complete mess" and an "electoral farce", as some polling stations did not even open, the counting in others took place by candlelight, some voters received several voter registration cards, etc. The team of Commonwealth observers considered that voting had been free from coercion, but stressed that there were "many complaints" about its organisation. A US statement was also very critical. During the days that followed, seven candidates, led by Fru Ndi, summed up the problems, denouncing many fraudulent practices. They announced that they would not recognise the results and called for the cancellation of the election. The ruling party, however, urged the public not to yield to the "provocation" and used the state media to call for calm, and the Catholic Church also called for the acceptance of the results.

The tension gradually subsided after arrangements were made behind the scenes. The Supreme Court rejected a request by the opposition to annul the elections, paving the way for the results to be announced, and they were published three weeks after polling day, by which time interest in the elections had faded.

In December, Biya carried out a *government reshuffle*, which gave the impression that he wanted to end the ambitions of some top figures in the regime. Several ministers changed portfolios. The influential Minister of Justice Amadou Ali became deputy prime minister in charge of relations with parliament, a ministry without power or resources. The powerful Minister of Territorial Administration and Decentralisation Amadou Marafa lost his job and was replaced by CPDM Secretary General René Sadi, often presented as a potential successor to Biya. At the same time as the reshuffle, in an indication the he did not distinguish between his party and the state administration, Biya appointed former minister of agriculture and rural development Jean Nkuete to be secretary general of the Central Committee of the CDPM. This appointment was announced on state radio as an extension of the statement about the government reorganisation. In December, the president chaired a cabinet meeting for the first time since July 2009.

There was no progress in the cases of the former ministers detained in *Operation Sparrow Hawk*, but some of them spoke openly for the first time. In July, the former minister of health, Urbain

Olanguena Awono, accused of corruption, issued an open letter denouncing a settling of scores against a background of political manipulation by the state apparatus. In October, Polycarpe Abah Abah, the former minister of economy and finance, declared in court that he had been in prison for almost four years on the basis of evidence that consisted of slander, lies and defamation. In December, the former secretary general of the presidency, Jean-Marie Atangana Mebara, published a book critical of Operation Sparrow Hawk, which spoke of an "abusive remand" and a "biased examination". All three had been detained since 2008 and each accused ministers of having plotted to kick them out of office, but no one dared to accuse Biya himself, which illustrated the fear that the president still inspired.

With regard to the fight against *corruption*, in November, the 'Commission Nationale Anti-Corruption' (CONAC) delivered its first report since its creation in 2006, focusing on just a few ministerial administrations. The results showed diversion of money at the national treasury and at the ministry of agriculture. CONAC also observed that, if the state put an end to the corrupt practices at the ministry of public works, three times as many roads could be built. The report pointed out the responsibility of several high officials, recommending prosecution, but no legal action was taken.

Foreign Affairs

The presidential election led to a cooling of relations between Cameroon and some of its main international partners, who seemed to want Biya not to stand for election. Several weeks before the elections, the *United States* caused offence by making statements hinting at a repudiation of the regime. On the occasion of the celebration of Cameroon's National Day on 20 May, US Secretary of State Hillary Clinton in a message to the Cameroonians urged the authorities to hold a free and fair presidential election. At the end of June, Assistant US Secretary of State for African Affairs, Johnnie Carson, paid an official visit to Cameroon and he also urged "free, fair and transparent elections". CPDM Secretary General Rene Sadi responded at a meeting in Kribi, saying that only Cameroonians would have the last word on the fate of their country. At the same meeting, the secretary general at the prime minister's office, Jules Doret Ndongo, also had harsh words for Cameroon's foreign partners. In July, the bishops of Cameroon, known for being close partners of the regime, recommended in a pastoral letter that the international community show greater respect for Cameroon's sovereignty.

Meanwhile, *France* remained silent in this debate, which was seen as a distancing from Biya, which was taken badly in Yaoundé. However, most Cameroonians had no doubt that Paris was still supporting Biya. French Minister of Cooperation Henry De Raincourt made a statement to the press during an official visit to Yaoundé on 1 July that France had no candidate for the elections.

Some tension and confusion were perceptible after the presidential elections. US Ambassador in Yaounde Robert P. Jackson made a statement noting irregularities at all levels on election day, which had given free rein to multiple voting. He also called on Elecam to demonstrate its independence from the ruling party, the CPDM, and for public resources not to be used in future for CPDM campaigns. This was in strong contrast to French Foreign Minister Alain Juppé's statement shortly after the polls that the elections had taken place "under acceptable conditions". Given the US position and the negative judgment of the Commonwealth on the organisation of the elections, Paris was obliged to re-examine this view and, a few days later, Bernard Valero, spokesman of the French foreign ministry, was less positive. He said that France had taken note of the result announced by Cameroon's Supreme Court confirming Biya's re-election, but that many irregularities had been found. "France hopes that steps would be taken to ensure that irregularities do not occur in the legislative and municipal elections of 2012," Valero added in his statement. In contrast to France, the US did not send any message of congratulation to Biya.

Biya replied to these criticisms in a speech delivered at the publication of the results: he claimed that the people of Cameroon had decided "freely and transparently" to assign him once again the responsibility of President of the Republic. In his end-of-the-year speech, he made a small concession by acknowledging some "shortcomings", but insisted that they had not been such as to jeopardise the outcome of the ballot, and that they would be corrected before the next elections.

Amid speculation about the cooling of relations with Washington and Paris before the election, Biya seemed to show his independence by making an official visit to *China* on 20–22 July, at the invitation of his Chinese counterpart Hu Jintao. Seven cooperation agreements (in the areas of health, education, vocational training, public lighting, culture and media) were signed on this occasion. Biya also had talks with several Chinese businessmen interested in investing in Cameroon, and several senior Chinese officials visited Cameroon later. Chinese Deputy Prime Minister in charge of Agriculture Hui Liangyu had already made an official three-day visit to Cameroon in January.

In June, tensions erupted on the border with *Gabon*: at least two people died and more than 2,000 crossed the border into Cameroon after being forcibly driven from the gold mining site in Minkébé (northern Gabon). Of those registered, 1,551 were from Cameroon and the rest from West Africa (Benin, Burkina Faso, Côte d'Ivoire, Guinea, Ghana, Mali, Niger, Senegal) and Chad. The expulsion order was made as a result of security issues and because, according to the Gabonese authorities, many workers had no identity documents. The Gabonese authorities further claimed that, in addition to criminal activity (poaching and illegal gold mining), Minkébé had also become a centre for illegal drug trafficking. Gabon President Ali Bongo said that, if there had been any wrong-doing during expulsion of the migrants' expulsion, it would be punished.

There were also incidents in late November on the border with the *Central African Republic* (CAR). The border was closed for four days at Garoua Boulaï (300 km east of Yaoundé) after an argument between a CAR soldier and a Cameroonian moto-taxi driver, which escalated into a shoot-out between CAR soldiers and Cameroonian police, although there were no casualties. The prefect of Nana Mambéré division, based 200 km away in Bouar, in west CAR, stayed in Garoua Boulaï for 72 hours to resolve the issue.

At the very end of the year, *Nigeria* decided to close the border with Cameroon because of the threat from Boko Haram, which was reported to have infiltrated northern Cameroon. A few days later, Cameroonian media reported that there had been calls for calm, tolerance and co-existence by imams in the mosques in the far north of Cameroon. They also reported that intelligence agencies believed that Islamic schools were being used for radical Islamic indoctrination and that surveillance was being undertaken by the Cameroonian authorities.

Socioeconomic Developments

There were no major economic events during the year. In January, the *IMF* office in Cameroon summed things up well in a document titled "Time for the lion to wake up?", which drew a portrait of the country's contrasts: although it has plentiful resources, its economic results do not match its economic potential because of the government's reluctance to adopt reforms. The IMF particularly underlined the lack of infrastructure, citing road transport tariffs in the order of $ 0.13 per ton-kilometre, compared with $ 0.05 in southern Africa and well below $ 0.04 in much of the rest of the developing world. The IMF estimated that the impact of improved infrastructure on real per capita GDP growth would be about 4.5%, and also noted the weakness of the *telecoms sector*: the two mobile operators charged very high prices and provided a poor quality of service for consumers. According to the IMF, if the quality and prices of telecoms services in Cameroon rose to match that found in Mauritius, real growth in GDP per capita would increase by 1.3% per annum, thus closing one-third of the gap between the country's current economic performance and its aspirations (Vision 2035) would be covered.

The 2011 budget was very similar to that of the previous year: it was set at CFAfr 2,571 bn (more than € 3.9 bn). The government targeted a GDP growth rate of 3.8% and an inflation rate of 3%, and predicted an oil price of $ 80 per barrel. The state intended to raise CFAfr 1,552 bn (€ 2.3 bn) in tax revenue, compared with CFAfr 1,440 bn (€ 2.1 bn) in 2010, and to earmark 59.1% of expenditure for public services, 26.5% for investment and 14.4% for debt repayments. It was counting on issuing government securities, on foreign borrowing and, of course, on oil revenue.

However, *oil production* continued to decline to an estimated 58,000 b/d, against 65,000 b/d in 2010. But there was some good news: the minister of mines said in November that heavy investment made in the previous three years, including in exploration, should increase oil production by 17% in 2012 to an expected 68,000 b/d. A few months before, in May, the Scottish group BowLeven, which holds an exploration licence covering a total area of 2,300 km^2, made a major discovery of oil off Douala, the economic capital and, in July, the state-owned 'Société Nationale des Hydrocarbures' announced the discovery by China's Yan Chang Logone Development Holding Company Ltd (a subsidiary of Shaanxi Yan Petroleum Group Corporation) of a field in the Zina and Makary blocks of the Logone Birni basin, in the Extreme North.

There was some small degree of progress on *infrastructure development*. Biya, who spent the entire election and post-election period in Kribi, in southern Cameroon, laid the cornerstone for the construction of the *deepwater port of Kribi* (which had been announced in 2000) on 8 October, just one day before the election. In January, the government had announced that it would borrow € 316 m from the Chinese bank Eximbank to finance the construction of the port (whose total cost was expected to be CFAfr 282 bn, about € 430 m), and construction work began at that time. A veteran of construction in Africa, the French company Razel, was responsible for the earthworks, and the China Harbour Engineering Company began the gigantic port engineering, including the construction of an embankment nearly 3 km long to guard against potential waves. In April, the works were halted for several days by angry villagers demanding compensation and relocation.

In the *mining sector*, some NGOs expressed concern about the mining law, asking the government to introduce regulations to control the use of local mineral royalties. There was also suspicion of fraud in connection with the diamond deposit at Mobilong (eastern Cameroon). In South Korea, the authorities opened an investigation into alleged corruption involving senior Korean officials and the Korean company C&K Mining, which had received a permit from the Cameroonian government to exploit the mine in 2010. The investigation was thought to hinge on the size of diamond deposits at the Mobilong field and on whether the mine's potential value had been intentionally exaggerated, as claimed by activists and experts, to cause a significant rise in the value of C&K Mining shares. Two Cameroonian NGOs demanded the suspension of C&K Mining activities in the country and a parliamentary investigation into the issuing of the mining permit. The South Korean investigation was expected to be concluded by the beginning of 2012.

In October, Cameroon was downgraded for the second time by the Council of the *Extractive Industries Transparency Initiative* (EITI) and failed to earn the status of compliant country. The Council estimated that the data from Cameroon in the EITI reports were under discussion, with questions being raised about their quality, and concluded that the EITI Secretariat, supported by the World Bank, should conduct further investigations. The embarrassment of the Council was apparent as it had to create a new status of "candidate close to compliance" specifically for Cameroon.

The crucial problem of *unemployment* persisted, despite a promise by the president that was headlined throughout the year. In

February, Biya promised to create 25,000 jobs in the public sector for young graduates in the coming year, but there was no doubt that the promise was directly related to the election. The government made efforts implement it and about 300,000 people applied for the jobs, but many of them complained about the lack of transparency and organisation and the commitment was ultimately not met. In early July, a strike by 2,500 health workers, recruited in 2007, exposed the real status of employment in the public sector: the workers were demanding payment of two years' unpaid wages and their integration into the Civil Service.

In May, the *Moroccan Attijariwafa Bank* bought 51% of the 'Société Commerciale de Banque Cameroun', the fourth largest bank in the country. The remaining shares (49%) were still held by the state of Cameroon. The Moroccan group said that it wanted to increase the rate of use of the banking system, which was very low (only 7% in Cameroon against 50% in Morocco).

In early July, Cameroon and France signed a second *'development contract debt (C2D)'*, amounting to € 326 m (about CFAfr 214 bn) over a period of five years (2011 to 2016). Initiated by France, the C2D is intended to cancel the debt of some countries by converting it into grants to finance development. As part of this programme, Cameroon had already received € 536.6 m (CFAfr 352 bn) for the period from 2006 to 2011. Cameroon was the first recipient in 2011 of French financial aid of France in sub-Saharan Africa and, according to French authorities, was the largest recipient of the C2D; 60% of the total C2D budget would benefit agriculture and rural development.

The *agricultural sector* received attention from the authorities during the agro-pastoral show held in January in Ebolowa (in southern Cameroon). Once a major rural affairs event, the show had not been held for 24 years and had been postponed several times in 2010. It brought together several hundred farmers, ranchers and companies for several days, and was, once again used by Biya as part of his election strategy: he visited it several times, accompanied by large numbers of attendants and many senior officials and media representatives. Recognising the exponential growth of food imports (for example, the expenditure of CFAfr 500 bn on imported flour, rice and fish in 2009 was seven times more than in 1994), he made many promises to the rural community, but no concrete measures were taken to solve the sector's pressing problems.

Cameroon was not immune to *land grabbing*, even though it went unreported in the media. In August, Biopalm Energy, a subsidiary of Siva Group of Singapore, launched a CFAfr 900 bn ($ 1.974 bn) palm oil project in southern Cameroon to be developed on 200,000 ha. It was claimed it would increase the annual production of palm oil to 80,000 tonnes over the first five years of production. Another agricultural company, Herakles Farm, based in New York, was also planning to develop some 60,000 ha of palm oil plantations in the southwest, but the project raised the ire of several environmental groups, among them the Australian Rainforest Rescue, which launched an online petition to put pressure on the Cameroonian government to reconsider the project, which it claimed was threatening some parts of Cameroon's unspoiled rainforest and the livelihood of the local population. There was no reaction from the government.

Cameroon in 2012

6 November was a historic day of great symbolic importance in Cameroon's modern history: President Paul Biya celebrated his thirtieth year in power. However, the year's most important political event was, without a doubt, the sidelining of Marafa Hamidou Yaya, one of the barons of the Biya regime, who was arrested and convicted of corruption. There were no major developments on the social and economic fronts, but the country was shaken by disturbing social unrest arising from specific events.

Domestic Politics

On 16 April, the 'Marafa soap opera' began with the arrest of Marafa Hamidou Yaya, the powerful former minister of territoral administration and decentralisation (2002–11) and former secretary general of the presidency (1997–2002), on suspicion of *corruption* related to the purchase of a presidential aircraft in the early 2000s, dubbed the 'Albatross Affair'. Two other men were arrested around the same time: former prime minister (2004–9) Ephraïm Inoni, and Yves-Michel Fotso, a prominent businessman. The three men joined around ten other former ministers imprisoned since 2006 as part of an anti-corruption drive called Operation Sparrowhawk, apparently a political purge from within the regime.

Analysts considered these arrests to be the latest episode in the *war for the succession (to the office of president)*, which had been playing out behind closed doors for a number of years. Marafa, reputedly close to French diplomatic and business circles, gave credence to this theory by making multiple political declarations in open letters. Indeed, he announced his presidential ambitions for the first time in letters published by a number of Cameroonian daily newspapers. He also tried to change his public image as a former power player

© KONINKLIJKE BRILL NV, LEIDEN, 2019 | DOI:10.1163/9789004401532_006

in the regime by revealing information about numerous corruption cases and even suggesting that President Biya should resign.

The Social Democratic Front, the main political opposition party, which was fast losing momentum, took sides in the internal succession struggle to replace Biya by publicly declaring support for Marafa and providing him with lawyers. Biya had never publicly addressed the issue of his succession. Shaken by Marafa's statements, the government and ruling party, the 'Rassemblement Démocratique du Peuple Camerounais' (RDPC), stifled Marafa's public declarations and ended any hope that he would escape his fate: In September, he was sentenced to 25 years in prison following an accelerated trial.

Another victim of *Operation Sparrowhawk* was the former minister of finance, Polycarpe Abah Abah; he had been in custody since 2008, but was arrested at his home in May, despite having permission to visit hospital. He was quickly sentenced to six years in prison for "aggravated evasion". Like Marafa, Abah Abah was detained under special conditions at the headquarters of the national gendarmerie, along with another former regime strongman, Titus Edzoa, considered one of Biya's rivals, who had been sentenced to 15 years' imprisonment in 1997. In October, he received a further 20-year prison sentence for corruption.

Another affair may also have been linked to the succession crisis: the implication in a corruption scandal of the president's eldest son, Franck, considered a potential successor to his father by some barons of the current regime, given that Biya (aged 79) was frequently portrayed as being in poor health. At the end of the year, Franck Biya, a discrete businessman absent from the political scene, was at the centre of a scandal that lasted for weeks. He was accused by 'L'Alliance pour la Défense du Bien Public', a previously unknown association, of having embezzled CFAfr 100 bn (around € 152 m) of public money in a financial operation dating back to 2006. In December, the One Cameroon Movement, an association of the Cameroonian diaspora in France, filed a complaint with the French 'Office Central pour la Répression de la Grande Délinquance

Financière', accusing Franck Biya of embezzling Cameroonian public funds. The Cameroonian authorities publicly denied his implication in the affair.

Municipal and parliamentary elections should have been held during the year, but were *postponed*. On 2 April, the terms of members of the RPDC-dominated National Assembly were extended by six months (renewable) and elections postponed *sine die*. Terms for parliamentarians elected in 2007 would have normally have expired on 21 August.

Prior to this decision, Elections Cameroon (ELECAM), the body in charge of elections, had announced in February that a completely new electoral roll would be drawn up, and called on all voters (nearly 9 m out of a total population of 19.4 m) to re-register. The background to this decision was that numerous cases of 'multiple voting' and registration of deceased persons had occurred during the presidential election in 2011. ELECAM also announced the introduction of biometric registration, a measure long called for by the opposition.

In mid-April, the National Assembly adopted a controversial new *electoral law*, which was heavily criticised by the opposition, who ultimately boycotted the vote. It emerged that many of the proposals made by the opposition during consultations with Prime Minister Philemon Yang had not been taken into account. Amongst the proposed measures that did not appear in the final bill were: a two-round presidential election (instead of one round), the reduction of the voting age from 20 to 18 years, and supplemental measures to ensure the security of ballots. The opposition also expressed its disapproval of the new law's removal of a provision allowing candidates' representatives to be present at polling stations. To express its discontent, the opposition refused to take part in the traditional national parade on 20 May.

The problem of *porous borders and national security* became apparent during a major poaching incident in the north of the country: Early in the year a team of approximately 50 poachers, probably from South Sudan, having crossed the CAR, ravaged the Bouba Ndjida national park, targeting elephants and their ivory. The Cameroonian government was severely criticised by international wildlife organisations for its failure to react. Under pressure from the media and international NGOs, Biya finally decided to send over 100 soldiers to the park. The poachers, accused by NGOs of having killed over 500 elephants, did not hesitate to attack the soldiers, even killing some of them. In December, over 600 soldiers were once again deployed in the Bouba Ndjida Park as a preventive measure to ward off a new incursion by poachers.

As is the case every year, on 1 October, the anniversary of the reunification of the British and French-administered Cameroons, members of the *Southern Cameroons National Council*, outlawed since 2008, called for the independence of the Anglophone part of the country. Approximately 50 people were arrested in a church in Buéa in the Southwest Region and others in Bamenda in the Northwest Region.

On the social front, there were many troubling events. The first occurred at the beginning of January: a robbery in the Deido neighbourhood of Douala, the coastal economic capital and a major urban centre, degenerated into battles with rocks and batons between moto-taxi drivers and local residents. These clashes led to the burning of numerous houses and quickly took on an ethnic tone. Hostile slogans were chanted against members of the Bamiléké ethnic group (originating in the West Region, but potentially the majority in Douala) many of whom were moto-taxi drivers. The governor of the Littoral Region, which includes Douala, was pelted with rocks when he attempted to visit the scene. Calm finally returned after five days. Local media reports of two deaths were denied by the local authorities, but the police presence and security measures were strengthened in Deido for weeks following the incident.

In mid-June, there were clashes between police and hawkers after an incident in the largest market in the capital, Yaoundé. Traders erected barricades and threw rocks at security forces reinforcements, who responded with tear gas. At least one person was killed. Numerous soldiers, police and gendarmes were deployed to the scene.

A news story about the abduction of a baby from the maternity ward of a Yaoundé hospital held media attention for weeks. The baby's mother, Vanessa, never recovered her child. 'Vanessa's stolen baby' filled headlines for a good part of the year, putting pressure on politicians and the government to comment. The regime's opponents denounced a human trafficking ring led by powerful elites, while others made Vanessa the symbol of injustice perpetrated upon the most vulnerable citizens. In March, members of the opposition were arrested and quickly released after attempting to protest against what had happened to Vanessa and the authorities were finally forced to sack the hospital's director. The young mother, who refused to leave the hospital, was finally removed by police in March.

In September, Biya, who rarely travels within the country, visited the north, which was hit by severe *floods* that caused dozens of deaths and displaced 50,000 people. Heavy rains, dilapidated dikes, and the decision to open the valves of the Lagdo dam caused the catastrophe. Biya ordered the release of CFAfr 1.5 bn (€ 2.3m) in emergency aid to the victims. Commentators believed that his visit was also an attempt to distract media attention from the Marafa trial, which was taking place at the same time.

Foreign Affairs

Several incidents widely relayed by the international media tarnished *the image of Cameroon*. The most important occurred during the Olympic Games in Great Britain, when eight Cameroonian athletes defected. According to media reports, they fled with the aim of staying in Europe for economic reasons. Their actions were the subject of extensive coverage in the Western media and created controversy in Cameroon: some commentators criticised

the athletes' lack of patriotism while others questioned and criticised Cameroonian policies that allegedly discouraged young
Cameroonians from believing in a better future in their country and
drove them to leave.

The French media focused several times during the year on cases
of arrests of homosexuals or presumed homosexuals, presenting
Cameroon as a backward-looking country that persecuted gays.

Some Cameroonian commentators were very critical of
Cameroon's loss in July of the CEMAC chairmanship due to the
new principle of rotation in CEMAC institutions. Antoine Ntsimi,
a former Cameroonian finance minister, who was in conflict with
President Bozizé of the CAR (where CEMAC headquarters are located), did not have his contract renewed and was replaced by Pierre
Moussa of Congo. This change was seen as a loss of Cameroonian
influence on the regional political scene.

Relations with *Nigeria* were quite satisfactory. The Nigerian government had until October 10 to appeal against the judgment of the
International Court of Justice that had granted the oil-rich Bakassi
Peninsular to Cameroon in 2002. The Nigerian Senate wanted the
dispute to be re-opened, arguing that the 2002 ruling was unfairly
based on an agreement dating back to the colonial era and that
the Peninsular's fate should be decided in a referendum monitored
by the UN. The government did not adopt this position, however,
and decided not to appeal, perhaps because of a proposal made
by Cameroon: according to the Nigerian media, Biya proposed
to the Nigerian authorities in May that the two countries should
jointly exploit the oil located along their common border in the
Bakassi area.

It is also likely that Cameroon's support for Nigeria in its fight
against the Islamist sect *Boko Haram* played a part in the Nigerian
government's decision. In fact, numerous Cameroonian media outlets reported the presence of the sect on Cameroonian soil, even
though there was no official comment on the issue. In February,
the president of the Association of Imams in Cameroon, Cheikh
Ibrahim Mbombo Moubarak, publicly expressed his concern that

Cameroonian Muslim leaders had allowed Boko Haram to preach in their mosques. The Nigerian and Cameroonian governments seemed to have worked together on this issue: in December, a newspaper revealed that the Cameroonian government had organised a series of arrests in border towns, including Amchidé, of people suspected of being affiliated with Boko Haram, who were subsequently delivered to Abuja.

In an extremely rare event, President Obiang of the Republic of *Equatorial Guinea*, with which Cameroon had several border disputes in the past, paid an official visit to Cameroon on 30 November. According to a joint press release following the working visit, the two countries agreed to expand and strengthen their cooperation in the economic, commercial, agricultural, public works and transport sectors, but observers speculated that Obiang had also come seeking Biya's support in the corruption case he faced in France.

In September, the city of Garoua-Boulaï on the CAR border was the victim of a mysterious attack that cost the lives of two Cameroonians. The attack was attributed to Central African rebels who came to free their comrades detained by the Cameroonian army. Four Cameroonians were abducted during the raid, but were freed in November after negotiations between the Cameroonian and CAR authorities. The government made no official comment on the incident.

Biya attended the 14th summit of the OIF in Kinshasa (DRC), where he had a meeting with French President François Hollande, their first since the latter's election in May. However, Biya did not attend the 15th conference of CEEAC heads of state, held in Chad in January, showing once again his blatant disregard for matters of sub-regional and African integration.

Socioeconomic Developments

The 2012 *budget* totalled CFAfr 2,800 bn (€ 4.2 bn), up 8.9% from the 2011 budget of CFAfr 2,571 bn (around € 3.9 bn). The total allocated to recurrent operating expenditures was € 2.6 bn, with € 1.2 bn reserved for investment. The remaining € 438.4 m was to finance Cameroon's internal and external debt. Internal revenue was projected at € 3.5 bn, with € 760.7 m in loans and grants. The contribution to the budget from oil revenue was set at € 864.3 m. The government's targeted economic growth rate was 5.5%.

Oil production was a little better than in the previous year at about 61,000 b/d (compared with 59,000 b/d in 2011). About CFAfr 510.1 bn (€ 777 m) was transferred as oil revenue to the public treasury (against CFAfr 572.7 bn [€ 872 m] in 2011). The state-owned 'Société Nationale des Hydrocarbures' (SNH) announced several discoveries in the Rio del Rey Basin, one by Glencore Exploration Cameroon Ltd in an exploration block, and another by Addax Petroleum, which said it had discovered a reserve of 20 m barrels, plus gas resources. In June, SNH signed an exploration contract with Dana Petroleum Cameroon Ltd for the West Bakassi block, saying that this was the first contract signed in the Bakassi area since the peninsula had been ceded back to Cameroon by Nigeria in 2008 in implementation of the 2002 judgement.

The Cameroonian authorities said that about 31 m barrels of crude oil transited by Cameroon from Chad to the oil terminal at Kribi (south) between January and October, compared with 34.85 m barrels during the same period in 2011. The state earned CFAfr 6.53 bn (€ 9.96 m) from transit rights, compared with CFAfr 6.95 bn (€ 10.6 m) the previous year.

During the budget session, the speaker of the National Assembly alluded to *bad governance* in the Cameroonian administration, calling for the budget be executed "with probity" and "an end to certain practices" such as percentages collected by ministers' collaborators for the granting of public contracts and the fictitious inauguration of unfinished public works projects.

Bad governance was also the subject of a report by the National Anti-Corruption Commission (CONAC): in an official report in November, the Commission revealed that Cameroonian banks were often "instruments of corruption, money laundering, and terrorist financing". One of the many files transferred to the justice system concerned the matter of CFAfr 2 bn (€ 3 m) of funding for an un-named "terrorist group". The CONAC also pointed to the sophisti-cated level of embezzlement and money laundering of public funds observed in the granting of public contracts and the management of large projects initiated by the government, citing the construc-tion of the Kribi deep sea port (South Region) for which 149 land owners received compensation of more than CFAfr 10 bn (€ 15 m). According to the CONAC, 44.7% of the land titles were granted after the site had already been taken over by the government for "public utility". The National Financial Investigation Agency reported the laundering of CFAfr 395 bn (€ 600 m) between 2006 and 2011.

In May, the World Bank demanded that Cameroon improve transparency in the *mining sector*, notably in the granting of per-mits. Since the adoption in 2001 of a new mining code, judged inadequate by NGOs, the government had granted two mining ex-ploitation permits and 160 exploration licences, mostly to foreign-owned companies.

In November, CamIron, the local subsidiary of the Australian company Sundance Resources Ltd, signed a mining convention with the government to exploit the immense iron deposit at Mbalam (South Region). The Chinese group Hanlong (attempting a takeover of Sundance) and the China Development Bank were financing the project, which needed over $ 5 bn in capital investment. In addition to the mine, a 510 km railway line would be built to transport iron ore to the port of Kribi, in the south of the country, which was still under construction.

On 14 August, Cameroon was officially admitted into the *Kimberley Process*, the international scheme to prevent the sale of rough diamonds from conflict zones. The Cameroonian govern-ment sped through the legislative and approval process under pres-sure from C&K mining. This Korean company, which was subject to prosecution for fraud on the Korean Stock Exchange for grossly inflating its diamond reserves, had been granted an exploitation permit for the Mobilong diamond deposit in 2010. NGOs expressed doubts about Cameroon's ability to trace its diamond exports, many of which originated across the border in the CAR, to Cameroon's artisanal mines.

There was some limited progress in *infrastructure* development. In June, when the country was severely impacted by an energy deficit, Biya officially launched the construction of a € 560 m hydro-electric dam scheduled to come online in 2017. The Memve'ele dam would have a capacity of 201 MW. It would be funded by the China ExIm Bank and the construction would be carried out by the Chinese Sinohydro Corporation Ltd.

In June, Cameroon and *China* signed a loan agreement valued at € 368 m to fund the construction of Cameroon's *first highway* linking the economic capital of Douala to the political capital of Yaoundé. The ExIm Bank of China would provide the necessary funding for the first phase of the project; total costs were estimated at CFAfr 284 bn (€ 432.9 m). The highway was projected to be 215 km long and take 60 months to build. The current road link between Yaoundé and Douala had just one lane in each direction and was regularly one of the deadliest in the country, with frequent accidents.

According to NGOs, hundreds of thousands of hectares of *land* were sold during the year to foreign companies by ministers, military officers, and presidential advisers in very opaque deals and in violation of national laws. Numerous national and international NGOs, including Greenpeace and the Oakland Institute, had particularly campaigned against an oil palm plantation by Herakles Farms, an American company planning to develop 60,000 ha in the Southwest Region. NGOs questioned the legality of the contract between the government and the company, as well as the risks to the local communities and primary forest in the area. In November, four members of a local NGO opposing the project were arrested and detained for two days. The government, including at least one minister targeted by the NGOs for signing the contract, made no official announcement regarding the agro-industrial project.

Cameroon in 2013

From the institutional point of view, Cameroon made significant progress with the creation of the Senate, an event that had been awaited since 1996 and a key factor in arranging the succession to President Biya, in power since 1982. The country also faced serious security problems: for the first time, the north witnessed abductions of French citizens, officially attributed to elements of the Nigerian-based Boko Haram movement, while armed groups of Central Africans carried out several murderous raids in the east. The crisis in the CAR also precipitated the arrival and temporary stationing of the French Army on Cameroonian territory, which gave rise to tensions.

Domestic Politics

As he had already announced in a speech delivered on 31 December 2012, President Paul Biya approved the implementation of an institutional reform that had been pending for 18 years: *the creation of the Senate* – a crucial element in the arrangement of his succession if he should die in office. According to the constitution of 1996, the president of the Senate should take interim responsibility in the event that the position of head of state should fall vacant. It was presumably in order to remain in control of politics that President Biya, who turned 80 in February, had repeatedly postponed the creation of this institution, which had been demanded with growing insistence not only by the opposition and the country's creditors, but also by members of his own party, the 'Rassemblement Démocratique du Peuple Camerounais' (RDPC).

The *first senatorial elections* were held on 14 April. As stipulated by the Constitution, the electoral college was composed of municipal councillors and had the task of electing 70 senators, 30 more

© KONINKLIJKE BRILL NV, LEIDEN, 2019 | DOI:10.1163/9789004401532_007

being appointed by the head of state. This ballot particularly mobilised the elites of the political parties, as the prospect of securing a remunerated appointment aroused the appetite of numerous ambitious personalities, thereby provoking internal dissensions. Tensions were strongest in the RDPC, the party leadership having thrust certain candidates aside to the benefit of others. Another contentious issue was the timing of the election: opposition leaders vainly called for the municipal elections to be held before the senatorial elections on the basis that this would have been logical, the municipal councillors' mandate having expired in mid-2012 before being extended by Biya.

Not surprisingly, the RDPC emerged victorious from the electoral process: of the 100 senators, 82 (of whom 56 were elected) came from its ranks. The remaining senatorial seats were shared by five other parties, notably the Social Democratic Front (SDF), the main opposition party, which secured 14 seats. The SDF chairman, John Fru Ndi, suffered a setback, having failed to be elected in his home region in the north-west of the country. Moreover, none of the senators appointed by Biya belonged to the SDF. In June, Marcel Niat Njifenji, a member of the RDPC, was chosen to become president of the Senate, thereby assuming the status of potential constitutional successor to the president. Having served as deputy prime minister in the early 1990s, 79-year-old Niat Njifenji had been director-general of the state power utility Société Nationale d'Electricité' (SONEL) for many years.

While the creation of the Senate succeeded in filling an institutional gap, it failed to resolve all the problems pertaining to the succession of the head of state. The actual legitimacy of the election of the president of the Senate, for instance, was weak, as was that of the president of the National Assembly (Cavayé Yéguié, 73, in office since 1992): officially administered by the electoral commission, 'Elections Cameroon' (Elecam), the senatorial elections were in fact under the direct control of the presidential administration. Furthermore, a *Constitutional Council*, although required by the

Constitution, had not been created. One of its functions would be to determine whether the head of state had become incapacitated. Knowing that he was expected to act on this point, Biya announced in his speech at year's end that a Constitutional Council would be created "within a reasonable period of time".

On 30 September, a few months after the senatorial elections, the *legislative and municipal elections* that should have taken place in July 2012 were finally held. They elicited very little participation and interest on the part of the majority of citizens, who, as in previous elections, doubted the impartiality of the electoral process. The opposition repeatedly criticised the authorities and the presidential party, accusing the government of – among other things – holding back the public funds necessary for financing the electoral campaign. Following the ballot, the opposition charged the RDPC with fraud, as in all preceding elections. Some 40 appeals were lodged, but they were dismissed by the Supreme Court. As a result of the vote, the RDPC won 148 of the 180 parliamentary seats (compared with 153 in the preceding elections of 2007). The SDF won 18 seats (compared with 16 in 2007). The 'Union des Populations du Cameroun' (a branch of the historical opposition party) won three seats, and the 'Mouvement pour la Renaissance du Cameroun', a party founded in 2012 by Maurice Kamto (a former minister turned oppositionist), took one.

The RDPC also obtained an overwhelming majority in the municipal elections, gaining control of 305 out of 360 municipalities (compared with 297 previously). Of the 35 political parties in the race, only ten secured municipal council seats. In the eastern and southern regions, the RDPC received the majority of votes in all municipalities and it also remained dominant in the centre of the country, where the capital Yaoundé is located. In the economic capital, Douala (Littoral Region), the RDPC carried Douala I, II, IV, V, and VI, leaving only Douala III to the SDF. In the north-west, Prime Minister Philemon Yang's home region and the stronghold of Fru Ndi, the RDPC took 19 municipalities and the SDF 15. It succeeded in ousting the SDF in Fru Ndi's native village of Santa. In the south-west, the RDPC was victorious everywhere except in Tiko, Kumba I, and Kumba II, which were won by the SDF. In the western region, traditional homeland of the opposition, the presidential party obtained a broad majority: apart from the Noun *département*, where the 'Union Démocratique du Cameroun', led by Adamou Ndam Njoya, won five municipalities, and only the town of Bafang went to an opposition party, namely the 'Union des Mouvements Socialistes', led by Pierre Kwémo. The SDF obtained only a relative majority in the municipality of Bafoussam I. The election results in the northern region brought no surprises: the RDPC and its ally, the 'Union Nationale pour la Démocratie et le Progrès' shared the seats.

Aside from these electoral events, political life saw little change: although still a taboo subject, the Biya succession remained the principal topic of concern among the political elites. A number of victims of the *anti-corruption campaign* 'Opération Épervier' (Operation Sparrowhawk) attracted attention, several of them having been presented as possible successors to Biya. Some made the headlines again on the occasion of their trials: on 2 October, the court sentenced the former prime minister, Ephraïm Inoni (imprisoned in 2012), to 20 years in prison for embezzling public funds and imposed the same sentence on his co-defendant, the former secretary-general of the Presidency, Jean-Marie Atangana Mebara (imprisoned in 2008). The former minister of basic education, Haman Adama, sparked a flood of comment upon leaving prison, having been released by the judicial authorities on 19 September after pleading guilty before the 'Tribunal Criminel Spécial' (TCS) and reimbursing the money she had been accused of embezzling. Upon her release, she thanked President Biya and immediately began campaigning for the upcoming legislative elections on behalf of the presidential party. Her release after more than three years in detention was interpreted as a way of securing support for the RDPC in the north, i.e. in her home region. It was also the home territory of the former secretary-general of the Presidency and onetime interior minister, Marafa Hamidou Yaya, who had officially fallen from grace in 2012. He had been sentenced to 25 years in prison in September 2012 for embezzling public funds, but continued to attract attention by publishing several letters from prison in the Cameroonian and foreign press. Expressing his views on the economy, politics and justice, his letters presented him as an alternative to the Biya regime, even though he had been one of its principal collaborators for 25 years. Known to entertain close ties to French as well as American business and diplomatic circles, Marafa was visited by US Ambassador Robert P. Jackson in June on the premises of the Secretariat of State for Defence, where he was imprisoned. In November, the Supreme Court rejected his application for a provisional release from detention. At the same time, two French lawyers, Jean-Paul Benoit and Jean-Pierre Mignard, a close friend of French President François Hollande, decided to take on his defence.

Even though Biya appeared to have retained overall control of the political system in the wake of the elections, he nevertheless encountered serious difficulties on the *security front*, with several alarming incidents now posing a threat to both the country and his own authority. The first such incident took place in the north, on 19 February, with the abduction of seven French citizens: the Moulin-Fournier family of three adults and four children, who were travelling as tourists in the vicinity of the border with Nigeria. According to the official version, they were detained by the Nigerian Islamist group Boko Haram before being liberated in April. In October, a French priest, Georges Vandenbeusch, was kidnapped in the same region and regained his freedom on 31 December. Official sources had little to say about these incidents. Even though the French authorities denied it, it subsequently became apparent that substantial ransoms had been paid to the abductors by Cameroon. Domestic and international observers also determined that these abductions had been organised in order to destabilise the Biya regime. Further unofficially leaked details showed that the Cameroonian security services suspected the involvement of a fringe group of the current regime that was hostile to Biya and included members of northern political elites. These incidents had at least one negative consequence for the country and its president: having received considerable media coverage in France (French Foreign Minister Laurent Fabius came to Yaoundé three times on their account), they left Western public opinion with the impression that Cameroon was a dangerous and insecure country.

On 27 December, Biya reacted by taking extensive measures to secure the borders with Nigeria, and also those with the CAR, as elements of armed Central African groups had repeatedly made incursions into Cameroonian territory. One measure taken was the creation of command posts for motorised rapid intervention battalions ('bataillons d'intervention motorisée') in Ngaoundere, Garoua, and Maroua, as well as at other, less important locations (Kousséri, Mora, Poli, Tibati). The security forces were also reinforced with newly created units. The recruitment of 4,400 men (2,300 for the defence forces, 300 NCO students for the gendarmerie, and 1,800 gendarmerie students), scheduled to begin in March 2014, was also announced.

Foreign Affairs

Though not readily apparent in public, relations between Biya and *France* seriously deteriorated over the months. A number of events caused the Cameroonian president to become increasingly wary of French government officials. The year had actually begun rather well: on 30 January, Biya was received in Paris by his presidential counterpart François Hollande. During this official visit, Biya met with prominent French businessmen (French companies still held a monopoly over many economic sectors in Cameroon, which also remained France's foremost partner in terms of security and defence cooperation). While in France, however, Biya was also confronted with an intensely hostile campaign by the major French media.

On the day of his visit to the Élysée Palace, 'Le Monde' published a column signed by Marafa and entitled "The post-Biya era must begin". Numerous media also highlighted the case of Thierry-Michel Atangana, a Franco-Cameroonian who had been detained in Cameroon since 1997 on a charge of corruption in conjunction with an affair that linked him to the former secretary-general of the Presidency, Titus Edzoa. Both had been sentenced to 15 years in prison in 1997, and were condemned to another 20 years in 2012. Siding with Atangana, the French media argued that he was being detained for political reasons and that Biya should release him.

Subsequently, the situation continued to deteriorate for the Cameroonian president. The Atangana case, which had long failed to attract the interest of the media and French officials, was mediatised several times by Paris and in May Hollande declared that the duration of Atangana's detention was "unacceptable". Biya suffered yet another indignity during the summit on Africa organised by the French presidency in December: he became the target of a verbal attack by Cameroonian citizens in the lobby of a large Parisian hotel, the 'Hôtel Meurice'. The incident was not well taken by the Cameroonian regime, which suspected the complicity of the French authorities. In spite of all appearances (Hollande publicly thanked Biya for his support on several occasions), the abductions of French citizens also placed additional strain on relations between Biya and his French dialogue partners. Yaoundé was shocked that France chose to declare the entire north of Cameroon a 'red zone' following the kidnapping of the Moulin-Fournier family and urged its citizens to leave the area immediately.

In spite of this strained situation, Biya authorised the *French Army* to land in Douala in order to proceed to the CAR within the framework of UNSC Resolution 2121: on 28 November, the French Navy's amphibious assault ship Dixmude arrived at the port of Douala with 350 soldiers and roughly 100 vehicles on board. On 5 December, the soldiers crossed the country to reach the CAR border. The French Army also established a temporary base at Ngaoundere airport (in the north). This presence gave rise to a number of problems, notably when the Cameroonian Army opposed the French Army's attempt to raise the French flag over the airport. Some Cameroonian media expressed surprise over the requisitioning and privatising of the airport by the French military. Others were alarmed at this presence, which brought back bad memories of the French colonial army's war against Cameroonian nationalists in the 1950s. The pro-presidential press, in turn, flatly accused France of planning to overthrow Biya as a follow-up to its intervention in the CAR.

Prior to the arrival of the French Army, Cameroon had already been directly affected by the crisis in the CAR. When the Séléka rebels seized power in Bangui, elements of the national army that remained loyal to ex-president Bozizé had indeed sought refuge in Cameroon. Bozizé himself officially went into exile in Cameroon on 25 March. Entering Cameroon from the east, he subsequently resided in Yaoundé. During the following months, after various units of the Rapid Intervention Battalion had been deployed on the border with the CAR, several clashes occurred with elements of the Séléka, including exchanges of fire with the Cameroonian Army over two days in mid-May. Another incident directly linked to the crisis in the CAR took place on 16 September, when Abdoulaye Miskine, the leader of the rebel group 'Front Démocratique du Peuple Centrafricain', was arrested in Bertoua (eastern Cameroon) and taken to prison in Yaoundé. A former ally of the Séléka, he was wanted by the new authorities in Bangui. Further outbreaks of violence occurred in November, when several other armed incursions and attacks on CAR citizens took place. In the early hours of 31 December, the Séléka also shot and killed five people, including two soldiers, in the village of Ondiki in the district of Kétté. Cameroon was also directly involved in the international reactions to the crisis in the CAR: on 10 October, following the adoption of resolution 2121, UN Secretary-General Ban Ki-moon sent his special representative in the CAR to Yaoundé. Subsequently, on 18 October, Biya took the further step of nominating General Martin Tumenta Chomu as commander of the armed forces of the AU's International Support Mission to the CAR, which, by the end of the year included 500 Cameroonian troops.

Socioeconomic Developments

The Cameroonian economy continued to fail to meet expectations due to its poor regulatory system. In his end-of-year speech, Biya himself said: "It seems that our efforts alone, no matter how laudable, will not suffice at their current pace to make Cameroon an emerging country in 2035. (...) In 2013, our growth rate stands at 4.8%, and thus below our forecast of 6.1%." At the beginning of the year, the World Bank estimated that poverty had increased in the poorest regions, situated in the north (North, Extreme North, Adamaoua) and east of the country.

The implementation of the annual *budget*, in particular, was plagued by serious delays and difficulties. Budgetary expenditures and revenues had both been fixed at CFAfr 3,236 bn, which represented an increase of 15.6% over the previous budget. Of this amount, CFAfr 2,912 bn were to come from domestic revenues and CFAfr 324 bn from external sources, as compared with CFAfr 2,280 bn and CFAfr 249 bn respectively in 2012. The government earmarked 60.7% of the total budget for direct operating costs, 29.6% for investment, and 9.7% for debt repayment. However, it was not until April that the budget began to be implemented, i.e. after a delay two months longer than in previous years. The situation did not improve thereafter: in November, implementation of the domestic budget for public expenditure in, for instance, the Ntem *département* (South) stood at only 4%. Similarly, as in previous years, there were numerous delays in the implementation of large-scale infrastructure projects due to lack of involvement by the state officials responsible, and also on account of administrative sluggishness and numerous other deficiencies. Biya himself explained at the end of 2013 that the delays in decision-making were causing "bottlenecks". He also said that it was necessary to "question the usefulness of certain project monitoring committees which are unable to take any decisions". An inquiry commissioned by the government to look into the years 2011–13 revealed that the state had signed project agreements without any reference to the state assuming responsibility for the costs of repairing access roads, compensating residents for infrastructural projects, project planning, and the like. The inquiry concluded that these omissions delayed the beginning of projects and led to disappointing results as well as additional costs.

The construction of a *bridge over the river Wouri* in Douala began after a long delay: on 14 November, during one of his rare journeys inland, Biya presided over the laying of the structure's foundation stone. The new bridge, with a projected length of 760 m, was expected to ease congestion on the only existing bridge, built in 1954, and was set to be completed by 2016. The cost of the project was estimated at CFAfr 120 bn (nearly € 180 m) and the 'Agence Française de Développement' agreed to provide finance in the amount of CFAfr 87 bn (roughly € 133 m), in the form of a sovereign loan of € 100 m and a € 33 m subsidy taken from the second Debt Reduction-Development Contract (C2D). The building contract was awarded to Sogea-Satom, a subsidiary of the French industrial group Bouygues. Various media claimed that France had pressured the Cameroonian authorities into rejecting a Chinese proposal. For some years, the government of Cameroon had been holding talks with China, which had commissioned the Gezhouba Group to look into the feasibility of the project. The latter had submitted a cost estimate of CFAfr 93 bn. China had planned to finance 85% of the costs, the Cameroonian share thus amounting to 15%.

In order to implement its infrastructural projects, the state was compelled in December to issue government bonds. This enabled it to raise CFAfr 80 bn on the Douala Stock Exchange (DSX). The funds raised from this call for capital were earmarked for construction projects, including the Memvé'élé Dam, to which CFAfr 23 bn were to be allocated. Further shares would go to the construction of the industrial port complex in Kribi (CFAfr 9 bn), the Douala-Yaoundé motorway (CFAfr 10.5 bn) and the Ring Road (CFAfr 7 bn) that was to connect the major cities of the north-east of the country. Somewhat more than 10% of the total budget was to finance the state's participation in business ventures.

The country's electricity supply, always unreliable and provided by the US-based AES Corporation, remained a matter of concern throughout the year. In mid-December, the government announced that it had approved an agreement to sell the Cameroonian assets of the AES Corporation to the British investment fund ACTIS for CFAfr 110 bn, a decision that attracted criticism from civil society actors and experts. The latter pointed out that the AES Corporation had kept none of the promises it had made in 2001 when it acquired a share in SONEL, 44% of which continued to be owned by the state: AES Corporation had promised, among other things, to invest CFAfr 1,000 bn of its own capital and to provide 68,000 new electrical connections per year, which it had failed to do.

Mobile telephone communications were still in the hands of two network operators, the French Orange SA and the South African MTN Group. A third operator, the Vietnamese Viettel Group, was chosen by the Cameroonian government in December 2012, but was still not operational.

Shortages also plagued the mining sector, on which the country officially relied to offset the drop in oil revenues, and it practically came to a halt. Large-scale projects (mining of an iron deposit in the south by CamIron, and of a cobalt/nickel deposit in the east by GeoCam) were at a standstill due to lack of motivation on the part of the promoters, as well as poor management and funding shortages. On 23 July, the US's Geovic Mining Corporation announced that it had signed an agreement with the Chinese Jiangxi Rare Metals Tungsten Holding Group for the sale of its shares in the GeoCam project, of which the Cameroonian state held 20%, at a time when strong suspicions of embezzlement were being voiced against the American company.

Only *diamond* deposits were being industrially exploited: according to the Ministry of Industry, Mines and Technological Development, Cameroon had exported slightly more than 2,414 carats of diamond since its admission to the Kimberley Process Certification Scheme on 14 August 2012. Handled by the Korean company C&K Mining, which held the mining concession in the diamond field of Mobilong (East), these exports generated profits of slightly more than CFAfr 281 m, of which 12.5% went to the state. According to the results of a survey conducted in July, there were seven small-scale diamond production zones. The National Permanent Secretariat of the Kimberly Process estimated that their production capacity amounted to about 5,000 carats per year.

As in 2012, the country's *oil production* experienced a very slight increase, reaching 24.2 m barrels (15.2 m barrels devolving to the state and 8.9 m barrels to the partner companies of Cameroon in the oil production sector), compared with 22.6 m barrels in 2012. Oil generated revenues of slightly more than CFAfr 832 bn (on a budgetary prediction of CFAfr 708 bn), compared with CFAfr 785 bn in 2012. Of this total revenue, the 'Société Nationale des Hydrocarbures' (SNH) reported that it had transferred CFAfr 553 bn to the public treasury, compared with CFAfr 510 bn in 2012. The state expected an increase in production for 2014, now banking on 30 m barrels due to the beginning of production in the Mvia oil field (in the Douala-Kribi-Campo Basin) in November 2013.

The level of *transparency in the extractive industry sector* remained low: in mid-May 2013, an American NGO, the Revenue Watch Institute (RWI), gave Cameroon a "failing" score for its governance of the oil sector. In its report, Cameroon ranked 47th out of 58 countries investigated throughout the world. It specified that the Cameroonians did not always have access to the information that was needed to ensure that the share of wealth issued from the natural resources of their country was fair. RWI also noted that the licensing process lacked transparency. It observed that there were few control mechanisms for monitoring the SNH, which collected the major part of the state's oil revenues, and estimated that only a part of the oil revenues actually found their way to the public treasury. In spite of these problems, and after several failures, Cameroon was recognised in August as a "compliant state" by the international committee of the Extractive Industries Transparency Initiative, indicating that it abided by prescribed norms of transparency.

The business climate was still poor, as Biya himself admitted in his end-of-year speech. Cameroon's ranking in the World Bank's global index "Doing Business" fell by six places, taking it down from 162nd to 168th place (out of 189 countries). The *fight against corruption* again failed to make significant advances and remained limited to a few spectacular arrests of individuals belonging to the ruling regime. In mid-January, the TCS, which came into existence in 2011, dropped a charge of embezzlement of public funds (CFAfr 230 m) against the former director of the now defunct Cameroon Airlines, businessman Yves Michel Fotso, who repaid the stolen money. For the first time since the launching of Operation Sparrowhawk, a prominent personality had officially returned the money that lay at the root of his legal troubles. Unlike Haman Adama, who went through the same process in September, Fotso did not regain his freedom: he was sentenced to 25 years in prison in relation to another matter. On 18 February, the director of the National Refining Company (SONARA), Charles Metouck, was arrested and imprisoned three days after being removed from his post. According to the Supreme State Audit, he was to pay around € 41 m in compensation for his bad management from 2007 to 2010. Even more important on the symbolic level was the arrest and imprisonment, on 10 June, of Iya Mohamed, who had been director general of Sodecoton (a public enterprise for cotton manufacture in the north of the country) for 29 years, president of the Cameroon Football Federation (Fécafoot) since 1998, and an eminent member of the RDPC. Although the arrest of this prominent personality from the north of Cameroon took place shortly after a defeat of the national football team, it was officially prompted by his management of Sodecoton, after he was accused of embezzling CFAfr 113 bn.

Few activities or changes took place on the social level. Between February and June, students staged *strikes at the University of Buea*, which is accustomed to such revolts. The students called for better studying conditions, the payment of research grants and the abolition of fees beyond the tuition fees (fixed by the state at CFAfr 50,000), etc. They also protested against the disbandment by the university's administration of the University of Buea Students Union, a powerful local student organisation. During these strikes, several outbreaks of violence occurred between the security forces and the students. In November, five students were sentenced to four years' imprisonment and fined CFAfr 800,000 for "inciting public unrest".

Several international and Cameroonian NGOs continued their protest, begun in 2012, against a *palm oil plantation* project on 73,000 ha in the south-west of the country. In June, two Cameroonian NGOs announced that they had brought a charge of corruption against Herakles Farms in the USA, the parent company of SG Sustainable Oils Cameroon Ltd, the company responsible for implementing the project. In late April, a report by the Ministry of Forestry and Wildlife accused the US company of using intimidation and corruption to acquire land. In mid-May, the Cameroonian authorities decided to suspend Herakles' activities, specifically for violations of the forest regulations, but this suspension was revoked on 29 May, without any explanation. At the same time, Greenpeace International and the Oakland Institute published a report claiming that employees of Herakles Farms had used corruption to obtain favours in Cameroon. In November, Biya finally granted the company 20,000 ha of land for a concession period of three years, at the end of which a very long-term leasehold agreement could be signed with the state.

Throughout the year, the EU urged Cameroon to ratify, before 31 October 2014, the interim *EPA* signed in January 2009, i.e. within the period stipulated by the EU. One organisation of employers,

E-Cam, expressed its opposition. Its executive members explained that the Cameroonians had not had the opportunity to defend their points of view and spoke of the EPA as a "weapon of mass destruction of Cameroonian enterprises". Quoting various studies, they also emphasised that the EPA would not only threaten the nation's still nascent industrial fabric, but also cause the Cameroonian customs to lose around CFAfr 100 bn a year.

Cameroon in 2014

The serious security crisis in the north of the country, characterised by repeated attacks and officially attributed to the Nigerian-based Boko Haram movement, was the main concern throughout the year, mobilising the army and raising controversies domestically and internationally. Linked to this issue, the relationship between the regime of President Paul Biya, in power since 1982, and France, the former colonial power, continued to deteriorate, though not in public.

Domestic Politics

After several abductions in 2013, the Far North region faced even greater security challenges: towns bordering Nigeria were targeted by armed attacks, which were officially attributed to *Boko Haram* and became increasingly frequent as the year progressed. In February, Nigeria announced the closure of a part of its border with Cameroon to stop Boko Haram from moving between the two countries. Towards the end of the same month, the village chief of Goumouldi was abducted and had his throat cut by presumed elements of Boko Haram. At the beginning of March, a military confrontation broke out near Fotokol between Cameroonian soldiers and armed men identified as Boko Haram members. Seven people were killed, including a Cameroonian soldier. Weeks later, reports revealed that numerous transfers of weapons were taking place between Chad and Boko Haram in Nigeria, through Cameroon. Other reports alleged that hundreds of young men, most of them Kanuri from Nigeria, were being recruited by Boko Haram and leaving their villages to join training camps, indicating escalating violence.

On 5 April, two Italian priests and a Canadian nun were abducted in Tchere, about 20 miles from Cameroon's border with

© KONINKLIJKE BRILL NV, LEIDEN, 2019 | DOI:10.1163/9789004401532_008

Nigeria. Boko Haram was once again suspected, although the terrorist group did not make any claim to responsibility. On 17 May, a Chinese worksite near the Waza national park was attacked; at least one Cameroonian soldier was killed and ten Chinese workers were kidnapped. Ten vehicles belonging to their company, China's state-run construction company Sinohydro, which was working on road maintenance, were also taken, although the worksite was protected by elements of the 'Bataillon d'Intervention Rapide' (BIR), an *elite unit of the army*. After these two events, President Biya decided to deploy more troops to the north. Official sources announced the addition of 2,000 soldiers, bringing the number of men present to about 3,000 in the three northern regions. The army divided the front line into two areas: the southern, held exclusively by the BIR, and the northern, held by the BIR in conjunction with several other army units. The Canadian nun and the two Italian priests were finally released in June, but the circumstances of their seizure and detention remained mysterious: no responsibility for their abduction was ever claimed.

In July, despite the military reinforcements, the *assaults* became more intensive and violent. A gendarmerie brigade was attacked in Bomberi, 5 km from the Nigerian border: a policeman was wounded and the attackers seized ammunition and a pickup truck. At the end of July, a dozen people, including the wife of Deputy Prime Minister Amadou Ali and a 'lamido' (a traditional chief), were abducted in two attacks on Kolofata, in the Far North Region, Amadou Ali's village. There were again numerous unresolved questions and disturbing details concerning this event: some reports said that some of the attackers were Cameroonians. A few days later, Biya dismissed several officers, including the commander of the Gendarmerie Legion for the north. No public reason was provided for these decisions, but informal sources spoke of the officers' potential complicity with the attackers.

A few weeks before, rumours had already started to circulate about the *identity of the funders, leaders and elements* of Boko

Haram, after a statement made by Cavaye Yeguie Djibril, the speaker of the National Assembly. Cavaye Yeguie, third in command in state protocol (after the president of the Republic and the speaker of the Senate), stated in the opening speech of the plenary session of the National Assembly that Boko Haram members were in high places in Cameroonian society. "We know them very well. Many of them are amongst us; some in hiding and others in active service, and in their hypocrisy do pretend to be supporting the state authorities to fight the sect; with the ulterior motive of destabilizing the state and setting it on fire," he said. Cavaye Yeguie was not publicly questioned on his assertions, but as a traditional ruler in the Far North Region and a man very connected in the region and the country, it was clear to everybody that he knew exactly what he was alluding to, though his motives were unclear.

A few weeks later, Anicet Ekane, of the opposition party 'Mouvement Africain pour la Nouvelle Indépendance et la Démocratie' (Manidem), and the Social Democratic Front, the main opposition party, in turn made statements pointing to the existence of a Cameroonian *armed rebellion acting under the cover of Boko Haram*. Unofficial sources in Biya's security services also referred to a rebellion sponsored by political elites from the north and members of the regime, talking of a 'Cameroonian Boko Haram' linked with the Boko Haram terrorist group in Nigeria. According to these sources, the aim of this Cameroonian rebellion was to destabilise Biya or even to overthrow him. Some members of the ruling 'Rassemblement Démocratique du Peuple Camerounais' also issued a public letter denouncing a "rébellion du Grand Nord". Because all of them were from the Lekié department in Centre Province, their statement gave rise to many criticisms and attempts at political exploitation of ethnic divisions, a tactic frequently used by the Biya regime. In October, the ten Chinese workers who had been kidnapped in June and the 17 people abducted in Kolofata, including Amadou Ali's wife, the lamido of Kolofata and some gendarmes, were all released, once again in very mysterious circumstances. In December, the archbishop of Douala, Samuel Kleda, publicly claimed that those who were attacking northern Cameroon were killing Muslims and Christians indiscriminately, and seeking to seize power, and that the Boko Haram issue was above all a political matter. However, no official made any public statement confirming this accusation, which was not surprising since the regime had always depicted Biya as a man who managed to keep Cameroon in peace. To publicly admit that the president was facing an armed rebellion would have destroyed the myth of "Biya, man of peace".

In the second half of the year, the Biya regime also had to deal with serious security threats at the border with the CAR, over which several people were arrested in August. Among them were Aboubakar Sidiki, president of a very small and unknown opposition party, the 'Mouvement Patriotique du Salut Camerounais', and Abdoulaye Harissou, a notary based in Maroua, member of the opposition party 'Union Démocratique du Cameroun' and known to be close to the former general secretary of the Presidency and former minister of interior Marafa Hamidou Yaya, who had been in prison since 2012. According to the authorities, Harissou and Sidiki were in contact with armed groups originating from the CAR. Harissou was accused of trying to recruit rebel factions in Chad, the CAR and Sudan to destabilise Cameroon, of having written speeches *calling for a popular uprising*, and of having sent journalists a document threatening state security. He was charged with insulting the president, hostility to the homeland and revolution, complicity in murder and illegal possession and carrying of weapons of war. He was detained in the Secretariat of State for Defence, the headquarters of the Gendarmerie, where other "very important prisoners" such as Marafa Hamidou Yaya were detained. However, these arrests did not prevent armed attacks along Cameroon's eastern border with the CAR. In September, clashes between armed groups and the security forces erupted in the area of Ngaoui Adamawa, and a businessman was killed in Saboua. Cameroon closed the border between the two countries. At the same time, an armed group attacked and kidnapped eight people in Garoua-Boulaï. Other battles took place in October between the Cameroonian army and rebels from the CAR who were trying to enter Cameroon via Garoua-Boulaï. The identity of the attackers was not officially announced, but according to some media, they may have been members of the armed group 'Front Democratique du Peuple Centrafricain' (FDPC) of warlord Abdoulaye Miskine, who had been in jail in Cameroon since September 2013.

At the end of November, the minister of defence announced that Cameroon had lost about 40 soldiers and killed almost 1,000 Boko Haram fighters. These figures were not verified by independent sources. There were generally serious *difficulties in obtaining reliable information* on what was going on at the battlefront. Unofficial reports also revealed numerous abuses, such as summary executions, committed by the army. Others indicated that the soldiers on the field were lacking resources. There were allegations of embezzlement of war funds and resources by the top brass in the Ministry of Defence. As in the Bakassi conflict, many years before, it clearly appeared that the war was a business opportunity for several actors.

At the beginning of December, the security situation finally drove Biya to take legal measures. Legislators voted on the draft of an *anti-terrorism law* prescribing the death penalty for all those guilty of carrying out, abetting or sponsoring acts of terrorism and allowing the punishment of people and companies found guilty of promoting terrorism, as well as various fines and prison terms for those who gave false testimony to the administrative and judicial authorities in matters related to terrorism. This law provoked anger within civil society and the opposition, who both accused the government of seeking to use the law to criminalise any opposition to Biya. Minister of Justice Laurent Esso replied that Cameroon would never be complicit with those whose only agenda was to destabilise the normal functioning of the state. Cameroon had not carried out any executions since 1997.

In February, Biya celebrated the *50th anniversary of the reunification* of Cameroon in Buea (South-West Region), three years later than planned. Although a cabinet reshuffle had been announced on several occasions throughout the year, it never took place. A few events that made the headlines showed the *lack of coordination* that existed at the highest levels of the state. For example, Minister of Secondary Education Louis Bapes Bapes was arrested in April and taken into custody without being dismissed from his post. He was released 24 hours later without explanation.

Foreign Affairs

The relationship between President Biya and *France*, already quite bad in 2013, continued to deteriorate. Biya finally gave in to the French government's pressure for the release of the French-Cameroonian businessman Thierry Michel Atangana. In February, on the occasion of the 50th anniversary of the reunification of Cameroon, Biya signed a decree granting remission to some individuals convicted for crimes including embezzlement of public funds. One of the articles of this decree seemed to have been tailored specifically for Atangana and his former mentor, Titus Edzoa, once general secretary of the Presidency and a former close collaborator of Biya. Both had been sentenced to 15 years in prison in 1997 and to a further 20 years in 2012 for corruption. Atangana and Edzoa were released and Atangana immediately left for France. Biya made no comment about French pressure.

In May, Biya attended a summit organised by France (in Paris) dedicated to the *fight against Boko Haram*, which brought together the presidents of Nigeria, Chad, Niger and Benin, as well as representatives of the USA, the UK and the EU. On this occasion, Biya publicly declared war on Boko Haram. Behind the scenes, bilateral relations were deteriorating: at the highest level of state, Cameroonian officials were sure that France was plotting against Biya and wanted to get rid of him and might even be supporting Boko Haram for that purpose. The messages delivered by media close to the Presidency provided an idea of this inside thinking: there were indeed regular accusations that France was a supporter of Boko Haram. In response, the French embassy in Yaoundé issued denials on several occasions. Cameroonian commentators noted that French President François Hollande visited Chad in July but did not go to Cameroon. At the end of the year, the tension was at its height, and many Cameroonians were now convinced that France was acting under the cover of Boko Haram. In late November, Biya went to the OIF summit in Dakar (Senegal). Although he had a meeting with Hollande there, reports noted that the Cameroonian regime disliked the French president's speech welcoming the "beautiful demonstration" of people in Burkina Faso that had ousted Blaise Compaoré from power. Some media close to the Presidency quickly established a link with the growing fears in Yaoundé and expressed regret that the French president praised popular uprisings.

One of the factors that further aggravated relations with France was certainly to be found in Biya's aim to diversify Cameroon's commercial partners and to forge closer relationships with *China* in particular. Since Biya's state visit to China in 2011, Exim Bank, the Chinese public financial institution that acts as the secular arm of Chinese investment abroad, had become Cameroon's largest donor, funding most of the country's major infrastructure projects: the Memve'ele dam, the deep water port of Kribi, the Yaoundé-Douala highway, the optic fibre network, etc. In 2012, China had become Cameroon's top donor and subsequently also its leading customer, being the destination for 15% of Cameroonian exports. Chinese Minister of Foreign Affairs Wang Yi made an official visit to Cameroon in January. More importantly, in October, the Cameroonian government signed an agreement with China for an equipment grant in the amount of CFAfr 2.5 bn for the Cameroonian navy.

Since *Chad* had become France's most important African ally, President Idriss Déby Itno was viewed with suspicion by the

Cameroonian authorities. In May, after the Paris summit on the fight against Boko Haram, Déby visited Cameroon, ostensibly for a "working and friendship visit" with Biya. On 27 November, the CAR warlord Abdoulaye Miskine, leader of the FDPC, a minor element in the Séléka rebel alliance, was released after being under house arrest in Cameroon for more than a year. This came in response to the release of the Polish priest Mateusz Dziedzic, who had been abducted mid-October in western CAR by FDPC fighters. Twenty-six other hostages, including 15 Cameroonians who had been detained since September, were released simultaneously. Media reports said that the President Denis Sassou Nguesso of Congo had played a mediating role in this exchange.

Socioeconomic Developments

The *economic cost of the war* was obviously heavy, even though there was no concrete assessment of how much was spent. According to unofficial sources, the war effort cost the government about € 1 bn in 2014. The trade, agriculture, transport, tourism and livestock sectors were the most affected by the armed attacks. Customs revenues dropped sharply, as the border custom posts in the Far North Region were closed down; they had preciously provided a monthly income of CFAfr 700 bn. At the end of the year, there were about 137,000 refugees from the CAR and 41,000 from Nigeria in Cameroon.

According to Prime Minister Philemon Yang, the GDP *growth rate* rose to 5.8%, a slight increase from 2013. It was also slightly higher than the CEMAC average of 5.7%. However, this result was actually lower than the 6% target initially set. According to Yang, this development was due to the sluggish global economic conditions and the security concerns in the north and east of the country.

Budgetary expenditure and revenues had both been fixed at CFAfr 3,312 bn, an increase of CFAfr 76 bn compared with the 2013 fiscal year. This small increase was intended to be used to support additional expenses, such as the salaries of a contingent of 25,000 new public sector recruits, the remuneration of traditional leaders and the costs of the recently created Senate. Expended revenues were CFAfr 1,985 bn from non-oil resources and CFAfr 718 bn from oil, an increase of CFAfr 13 bn overall. The government planned to issue bonds worth CFAfr 280 bn and also expected CFAfr 658 bn in loans and donations. The government earmarked CFAfr 2,01 bn (62.1% of the budget) for direct operating costs, CFAfr 1,000 bn for investment and CFAfr 302 bn for debt repayment (compared with CFAfr 314 bn in 2013).

For the third year running, the country's *oil production* increased, reaching 27.5 m b/d, compared with 24.2 b/d in 2013. This increase was due to the intensification of exploitation of a major offshore field and to the commissioning of three new fields. *Gas exploitation* was up by 124% according to the 'Société Nationale des Hydrocarbures'. The improvement was due to the Sanaga South field, whose production was constantly growing, and to the Logbaba field, which was exploited by Rodeo Development, a subsidiary of the British Victoria Oil & Gas. The gas potential was also revalued upward from 144 bn m^3 to 154 bn m^3. This increase of 10 bn m^3 followed new exploration work in some petro-gas fields by operators under contract to the state.

Pushed by the IMF and the World Bank, Biya had to take unpopular measures: he decided to revise upwards the *prices of fuel and cooking gas* early in July, making a litre of super cost CFAfr 731, 14.2% up from the previous CFAfr 650; these prices had been frozen by the government since 2008. The cumulative loss to the state amounted to CFAfr 1 357 bn (€ 2 bn) over the years, according to the government.

To mitigate the effects of this measure, Biya increased the *salaries of civil servants* by 5%. This decision, following the increase in fuel prices at the pump, was expected to cost about CFAfr 30 bn (€ 45 m) annually and affected more than 200,000 people. The government also reviewed the fuel price structure, reducing *inter alia* the special tax on petroleum products ('taxe spéciale sur les produits pétroliers'; TSPP) and some taxes paid by trucks. The fall in TSPP would impact on the public finances to the tune of about CFAfr 15 bn. In late July, the *guaranteed minimum wage* ('Salaire Minimum Interprofessionnel Garanti'; SMIG) was also increased by about 30%, from CFAfr 28,216 to CFAfr 36,270 (€ 55) per month. The last SMIG increase occurred in June 2008 (when it had been CFAfr 23,000 [€ 35]), after the riots of February 2008.

In early December, Biya launched a CFAfr 925 bn three-year *'emergency plan'* (2015–17), financed by Deutsche Bank, 'Banque Gabonaise et Française Internationale', Ecobank, Atlantic Bank and Standard Chartered Bank. Through this 'emergency plan', the government planned to invest in various projects in agriculture and livestock (seed distribution, slaughterhouses and cold storage), health (general hospitals and rehabilitation of technical facilities), social housing (1,000 units to be built in the country's ten regions), infrastructure (roads, construction of police stations and border posts, water supply in cities and in rural areas, public lighting in Yaoundé and Douala ...).

In July, the National Assembly and the Senate succumbed to European pressure and approved the *ratification of the interim EPA* with the EU. This agreement, signed by the government in 2009, provides for a tariff dismantling over 15 years between Cameroon and the EU, as well as the liberalisation of 80% of imports from Europe. Some Cameroonian employers denounced this agreement, saying it was one-sided and emphasised that the government had estimated the losses for Cameroon to be about CFAfr 1,500 bn (€ 2.3 bn) in 2020 and CFAfr 2.5 bn (€ 3.8 bn) in 2030.

Some changes occurred in (former) *parastatal* companies. In September, the national electricity company SONEL changed its name to Energy of Cameroon (ENEO). Owned since 2013 by the British Actis, ENEO had a portfolio of more than 900,000 customers and an installed capacity of 935 MW and was employing 3,600 people. The company was planning to invest CFAfr 170 bn (€ 260 bn) over the next five years. In September, the government issued a 3G license to the national telephone company Cameroon Telecommunications (Camtel) and to MTN (South Africa), Orange (France) and Nextell (Vietnam). This decision put an end to Nextell's monopoly on 3G. Nextell, which launched its operations only in September 2014, asked in vain for the extension of its previously agreed privilege beyond the expiry date of 31 December. With about 1 m subscribers, Camtel had only a 5.7% market share in the Cameroonian telecoms market (land line and mobile), behind MTN (57%) and Orange (37%).

An important change on the *mining* front was the announcement in October by the Anglo-Australian mining group Rio Tinto that it would relinquish ownership of its share in Alucam at the end of 2014. Created by the French group Pechiney, Alucam had produced aluminium since 1957. Rio Tinto had held 46.7% of its capital since 2006 (in equal shares with the State of Cameroon, the remainder being held by employees and the 'Agence Française de Développement'). Rio Tinto explained that Alucam's business plan was no longer in line with its strategic priorities, but that it would assist the government in finding a buyer and would maintain technical and administrative assistance contracts. This decision came as Alucam had started several development projects, including the extension of its aluminium factory in Edea to increase capacity to 300,000 tonnes per year. This extension was linked to the development of the Lom Pangar dam and the Nachtigal dam. It was also planning to set up another aluminium factory near Kribi to produce 800,000 tonnes from 2021. This project was conditioned by the construction of the Song Mbengue dam (930 MW). With 570 employees, Alucam had an annual production capacity of 100,000 tonnes. All ambitious expansion plans were seriously endangered by the Rito Tinto move.

The *anti-corruption campaign* 'Opération Epervier' (Operation Sparrowhawk) produced few headlines. There was only one major arrest: Gervais Mendo Ze, former director of Cameroon Radio

Television for 17 years and former minister for communication, was arrested in November. Sacked from the government in 2005, he had been repeatedly under the spotlight for all kinds of alleged wrongdoing during his time in office. One detainee convicted of corruption, the former Cameroonian ambassador to the USA, Jerome Mendounga, died in custody in November. He had been imprisoned in 2009 and convicted of embezzlement in 2012 in the case of a purchase of a presidential plane called 'Albatros'.

Cameroon in 2015

On the political front, a minor cabinet reshuffle took place at the end of the year. Security remained a major problem in the Far North region with armed attacks and suicide bombings attributed to the Nigerian-based Boko Haram movement, which had killed hundreds of people. The East region was also affected by insecurity, with regular incursions by armed gangs, probably coming from the CAR. Cameroonian security forces were accused of human rights violations in the Far North. On the economic front, the country was able to adjust well to the fall in crude oil prices, but corruption scandals continued. Analysts were becoming increasingly concerned about the rapid increase in the country's debt.

Domestic Politics

Boko Haram's insurgency in the Far North region dominated the news throughout the year. For the first time, the leader of the group, Abubakar Shekau, threatened President Paul Biya directly in a 17-minute video posted on 5 January: "Paul Biya, if you do not put an end to your evil plan you'll be entitled to the same fate as Nigeria (...). Your soldiers can do nothing against us," Shekau said. As in 2014, Boko Haram engaged in guerilla style warfare, deploying small raiding forces, but they also operated as an army capable of deploying hundreds of fighters armed with heavy artillery (including rockets and tanks). On 17 April, more than 100 Boko Haram fighters stormed the town of Bia, killing 16 civilians. In a report published in September, AI estimated that, in the period from mid-2014 to mid-2015, Boko Haram had attacked dozens of towns and villages, killing nearly 400 civilians, burning hundreds of homes and looting livestock. Cameroonian security forces also committed violence in response. AI accused them of numerous *human rights violations*,

© KONINKLIJKE BRILL NV, LEIDEN, 2019 | DOI:10.1163/9789004401532_009

including summary executions. The report documented that the security forces attacked villages, destroying homes, killing civilians and arresting more than 1,000 suspects, including children as young as five. About 84 children were unlawfully detained for six months at a children's centre after security forces descended on the city of Guirvidig. At least 25 people died in custody, and there was no news of at least 130 others who had been arrested. The Cameroonian authorities did not respond to letters from AI expressing serious concern.

In July, terrorism gained further prominence with a first *suicide bombing* in Fotokol. The bombing was followed by several more, all in markets in the Far North region: Mora, Kolofata and Kaliari were among the affected cities. These attacks were attributed to Boko Haram, although the terrorist group did not claim responsibility and some of the incidents occurred far from Boko Haram's usual area of activity. In Maroua, capital of the Far North region and located 400 km from the Nigerian border, 33 people were killed in several suicide bombings in late July. In December, two suicide attacks killed at least four people at Waza, a town bordering Nigeria and Chad. These attacks appear to have been committed by children, teenagers or socially vulnerable women, who were unwittingly carrying the explosives, some of which were triggered by remote control. After the first suicide bombings, committed in Fotokol by two women wearing burqas, the governor of the Far North region decided to ban the garment.

Terrorism in the north had an impact on major cities in the south. After the suicide attacks in Maroua, inhabitants of Yaoundé and Douala also became afraid. Controls on roads and at bus stations nationwide were tightened by police, primarily in Yaoundé and Douala. In Yaoundé, in the popular neighbourhood of Briquetterie, known for its large Muslim community, the police raided houses and mosques in July. According to local newspapers, dozens of people were arrested. Minister of Communication Issa Tchiroma Bakary said that these sweep operations had led to the arrest of many suspects in several regions of the country. *'Vigilance committees'* made up of residents were set up in some localities to fight the terrorist group by providing security forces with information. Local authorities equipped the committees with binoculars, torches, mobile phones, etc. Some members were armed with clubs and machetes. Their role was hailed by President Biya in his end-of-year address: he spoke of the "legitimate exercise of civil defence" and portrayed such committees as "models" for the nation. Worried voices asked what these committees would become after the end of the 'war'.

Actions by Boko Haram and indiscriminate retaliation by the army both had severe humanitarian consequences: the number of IDPs grew dramatically. The UN Office for the Coordination of Humanitarian Affairs estimated that they numbered 117,000 in March. Many had abandoned their farms, which directly aggravated malnutrition in an area that was still recovering from a decade of periodic drought. In addition, according to UNICEF, by the end of the year, only one of the 135 schools that had closed in 2014 because of the conflict with Boko Haram had re-opened.

On 28 February, thousands of Cameroonians demonstrated in Yaoundé to denounce the terrorist group's atrocities and to support the Cameroonian army. However, the march, officially organised by a few journalists and a private newspaper editor, did not receive unanimous approval. Critical observers denounced political exploitation, if not outright manipulation, by a few regime members. Some ministers had in fact joined the march, including Minister of Defence Edgard Alain Mebe Ngo'o, Minister of Labour Grégoire Owona, and Tchiroma. It should be noted that the authorities in Cameroon rarely allow *demonstrations*, much less participate in them. Some local analysts claimed that the event, presented by its organisers as a civil movement, was in fact secretly financed by the minister of defence.

There was general questioning of the real identity of the Boko Haram fighters. The idea that the terrorist group concealed Western interests became increasingly widespread among the population.

Professor Jean Emmanuel Pondi of the International Relations Institute of Cameroon, who was not known to be close to the Biya regime, publicly stated the view that the attacks on Cameroon were related to its wealth, which "some countries want to seize" and he also spoke of a plot to destabilise the country.

Apart from the Far North region, other areas of the country also faced significant security issues throughout the year. In Adamawa, armed gangs, allegedly coming from the CAR, conducted dozens of *kidnappings* for ransom throughout the year. Between July and December, the authorities counted 76 hostage takings in the region. The departments of Vina and Mbéré were the most frequently targeted and several raids by armed gangs were also reported in the East, on the border with the CAR. Seventeen people, including a mayor and four traditional chiefs, were abducted in March in the village of Babio, close to Garoua Boulaï. According to the Ministry of Communication, the hostages were taken to the CAR.

On 2 October, Biya finally carried out a minor *government reshuffle*, which had in fact been expected since the legislative and municipal elections of September 2013. The president kept Philemon Yang as prime minister but Minister of Defence Mebe Ngo'o was replaced by Joseph Beti Assomo, formerly governor of the Littoral region. Mebe Ngo'o, who was said to have grown up in Biya's house, was known for his extravagant life-style – his official motorcade was similar in size to the president's, for example – and he was also suspected of using the army's human and material resources for personal purposes, while the soldiers fighting against Boko Haram were experiencing difficult conditions on the ground. On 9 September, about 200 soldiers wearing UN blue helmets marched over 4 km from their base in Ekounou, a popular area of Yaoundé, through the town centre towards the army headquarters, demanding their unpaid bonuses. They were part of the 1,260 *Cameroonian contingent with the UN mission in the CAR* (MINUSCA). This was the first time that soldiers had marched in the streets of the capital. The government deployed heavily armed troops to block streets and impede their passage, but the minister of communication stated that the contingent would quickly be paid. Mebe Ngo'o's removal was therefore popular, but also matched other calculations: Known for lavishly funding numerous private media outlets, Mebe Ngo'o seemed in fact to have been demoted by Biya because of his supposed presidential ambitions (a fate shared by others from Biya's inner circle). A few weeks later, Mebe Ngo'o, who was shifted to the significantly less important Ministry of Transport, was summoned by the military court to answer several cases of corruption filed against him. Meanwhile, his successor symbolically spent 31 December in the Far North with the troops in Kidimatari. Mebe Ngo'o had never visited the front line.

Biya, aged 82, still showed no desire to leave the presidency. On the contrary, many signs indicated that he was planning to stand for *re-election in 2018*. For example, numerous 'motions of support' came from members or elites of the ruling party, calling for his re-election. In the past, Biya had always used these expressions of support published by the state media to justify his decision to stand again for election as president. The population, for their part, sarcastically noted that, during Biya's traditional speech on 31 December, Cameroon experienced a huge power outage as he was speaking about the need for adequate and permanent sources of energy. The minister of energy announced that the power cut was due to crows nesting on connections and electrical installations.

Foreign Affairs

On 21 February, French Foreign Minister Laurent Fabius came for a short official visit to Cameroon. Biya received him in the context of tense relations between the two countries, as was the case in 2014. Officially, Fabius came to Yaoundé – staying less than 24 hours – to express the support of *France* for Cameroon in the fight against Boko Haram. Some Cameroonian commentators, however, felt that this visit was primarily intended to rebut allegations that France had connections with and was supporting Boko Haram, and wanted to use the terrorist movement to destabilise Cameroon. During his visit, Fabius had to repeat many times that France was a friend of Cameroon

On 3 July, French President François Hollande made a state visit to Cameroon to meet with Biya, the first visit by a French president since 1999. However, the visit lasted only a few hours, showing that the relationship between Hollande and Biya was still complicated. The visit was part of the French presidency's campaign for the UN conference on climate change (COP21), which was hosted by France a few weeks later, in December. Hollande needed the votes of African countries for the adoption of the forthcoming Paris agreement. During his visit, Hollande also met with leaders of political parties represented in the National Assembly, without distinguishing between opposition parties and the presidential party. At a joint press conference with Biya, he made an important statement that went almost unnoticed in France but was much commented on in Cameroon: the French president implicitly recognised *the repression by the French army* in Cameroon in the 1950s of the 'Union des Populations du Cameroun' (UPC), a political party calling for independence. In the late 1950s, tens of thousands of UPC members had been massacred by the French army, including the UPC leader, Ruben Um Nyobe, who was killed in 1958. The repression continued after independence in 1960 and was led by the Cameroonian army, under the supervision of French officers. Hollande spoke of "tragic episodes" and of "repression", and gave assurances that he wanted the archives to be opened to historians. Thus, Hollande became the first French president to speak of this period in the history of the two countries. Until then, French officials had always denied the extent of French repression and, in 2009, the then French Prime Minister François Fillon had publicly refused to admit that the French had killed people in Cameroon. Hollande's statement broke a taboo, observers noted. According to some Cameroonian analysts (and also noted in the French press), the French authorities' new attitude was due to the rise of anti-French sentiment in Cameroon, the increasing influence of China, which had won numerous large public contracts in Cameroon, and France's desire to reclaim its diminishing influence/control. The Cameroonian historian Achille Mbembe said that Hollande was seeking to eliminate grievances against France without having to pay anything.

A television channel based in Yaoundé, Africa Media, was sealed off after airing accusations that France and the USA were supporting Boko Haram. The 'Conseil National de la Communication' (CNC) justified its decision by claiming that some guests of the channel from politics, academia and civil society had openly and repeatedly accused Paris and Washington of supporting Boko Haram. The presenters of some of the incriminated programmes were also suspended for six months by the CNC.

In November, Cameroon agreed that the USA would establish a drone base in Garoua (North), and accepted the deployment of 300 US soldiers. The contingent was officially sent to conduct airborne reconnaissance operations in the region, to help fight terrorism and to provide intelligence to the multi-national task force being set up to fight Boko Haram. The USA gave assurances that their troops deployed in Cameroon were armed only for their own protection and security, and that they did not have a combat mission. Off the record, some Cameroonian officials expressed concern, admitting that Cameroon would not have the means to control their activities. Some residents of Garoua were convinced that the USA was in fact interested in exploiting oil reserves believed to be situated along Cameroon's border with Chad.

To everyone's surprise, the *Chadian army* entered Cameroon on 17 January to fight Boko Haram. Many Cameroonians were sceptical about this operation, as the role of Chad in the region had been at least ambiguous: Chadian President Idriss Déby Itno had at one point been suspected of himself having links with Boko Haram. It was also widely known that Déby and Biya did not have a good relationship. In early November, Chad suddenly withdrew its troops from Cameroon without any official announcement.

In July, the new *Nigerian President Muhammad Buhari* made a two-day visit to Cameroon. Biya greeted him on his arrival at Yaoundé airport. The two heads of state held talks about ways to defeat Boko Haram. This meeting took place two months after a state visit by the Nigerian president to Chad and Niger. Analysts said that the visit would help erase the climate of mistrust between Cameroon and Nigeria, after years of relations strained because of the border dispute over Bakassi. Cameroon had for some time been accused by Nigeria of dragging its feet over tackling Boko Haram and Cameroon complained of Nigeria's refusal to grant Cameroonian forces the right to pursue them onto Nigerian soil. It should be noted that Biya did not attend Buhari's inauguration in May.

Socioeconomic Developments

Cameroon suffered from the *drop in world oil prices*, but the economy showed remarkable resilience. Indeed, the fall in oil revenues was partially offset by an increase in production. The start of production at the Bojongo field and the reactivation/optimising of mature fields in the Rio del Rey basin (Inter-Inoua Barombi, Barombi Northeast and Padouk) were part of this strategy. According to the 'Société Nationale des Hydrocarbures' (SNH), production reached 102,586 b/d on 21 April, a level last achieved in 2002, and 35 m barrels were produced over the year. On 31 December, oil and gas production was up about 26% year-on-year. Gas production reached 12.5 bn ft^3. The SNH paid the treasury CFAfr 378,536 bn – substantially more than the budgeted annual target of CFAfr 264,25 bn.

The *state budget* increased slightly over the budget for 2014: revenues and budgetary expenditure were set at CFAfr 3,746 bn, compared with CFAfr 3,312 bn in 2014, an increase of 13.1%. Investment represented CFAfr 1,150 bn, up from CFAfr 1,000 bn in

2014, operating costs were estimated at CFAfr 2,159 bn, (an increase of CFAfr 150.7 bn compared with 2014) and the public debt service was CFAfr 302.8 bn. The government expected a GDP growth rate of 6.3% and an inflation rate of around 3%. While GDP had been expected to rise to 6.1% in 2014, it reached only 5.1%, according to the IMF. The Ministry of Finance deemed growth insufficient to signal a real takeoff of the economy and to reduce poverty, estimating that Cameroon had the potential to reach annual rates above 10%.

One of the main barriers to growth lay in the recurrent shortcomings of the *port of Douala*, entry and exit point for 95% of imported and exported goods. Ship-owners constantly assessed Douala as one of the world's most disastrous port sites, citing the silting up of the access channel and the absence of modern infrastructures to cope with the intensity of traffic. The passage of goods took 22 days, i.e. five times longer than at the port of Durban (South Africa), according to a World Bank study.

To reverse the trend, there were high expectations concerning the *deep water port* that was being built in Kribi, in the south of the country. Some platforms were already operational. On 26 August, Prime Minister Philemon Yang announced that a consortium of the French companies Bolloré and CMA CGM and the China Harbour Engineering Company had been awarded the operation of the container terminal of the port of Kribi. Another consortium made up of French group Necotrans and the Cameroonian Kribi Multi Port Operators won the management of the multi-purpose terminal. Operations were planned to start at the port in the second quarter of 2016. These projects were expected to create 10,000 direct jobs. Cameroon was projected to earn 1.5% of growth each year, once the complex was fully operational, according to official – and optimistic – projections that saw the new port as a 'hub' capable of capturing maritime traffic through the Gulf of Guinea.

Insecurity in the Far North and in the East also impacted on the economy and government finance: the maintenance of 6,000 men in 14 bases was, of course, expensive. Yaoundé also had to provide the fuel for the 2,500 Chadian soldiers fighting alongside Cameroonians. *Corruption* was another major constraint on economic development: Cameroon remained one of the most corrupt states in the world. TI placed it at the head of the most corrupt African countries, with only Liberia rated worse. The public 'Commission Nationale Anti-Corruption' (CONAC) in a report on 2013 released in 2015 pointed to the issuing of false pay slips, the inflation of officials' salaries and pensions, the processing of false driving license, fraudulent billing for services, etc. The Commission noted numerous problems in delivering false patents, and the issuing of false tax stamps by illicit stamp machines, even within Directory General of Taxes. The CONAC also highlighted the opacity of the 'Bureau de Gestion du Fret Terrestre', which, according to the CONAC president, had "become a state within the State". The government did not take any major measures to fight corruption: there was no notable progress on 'Operation Epervier', launched by Biya in 2006 to fight corruption at the official level, apart from court rulings against two 'big men'. A special criminal court sentenced former finance minister Polycarpe Abah Abah to 25 years in prison for embezzling CFAfr 6 bn to buy houses and cars. Abah Abah, formerly a powerful minister, in jail since 2008, appealed his sentence. The former general manager of the state-owned bank 'Credit Foncier du Cameroun', Joseph Edou, and his deputy were sentenced to 15 years in prison for embezzlement.

The *business climate remained poor*, and Cameroon plummeted ten places in the World Bank's 'Doing Business 2015'. Several reports also stated that Cameroon, with 40% of its territory still forested, had failed to make progress in tackling illegal logging since the conclusion, in 2010, of a Voluntary Partnership Agreement between Cameroon and the EU. According to the EU, this agreement was intended to provide a legislative framework within which to detect and ensure the traceability of timber; put in place government and independent verification procedures to certify that all timber exports from Cameroon to European markets had been procured, felled, transported and exported legally, in order to provide a basis for the legal management and exploitation of the Cameroonian forests; and reinforce the application of forestry regulations and governance. But a report by an independent auditor financed by the EU showed that none of the logging companies working in Cameroon, including European companies, were compliant with Cameroonian laws.

To improve the situation, the government launched its first *Eurobond* at the end of the year: € 750 m (CFAfr 462 bn), issued at a yield of 9.5% for a weighted average life of ten years. This loan was part of a plan to mobilise CFAfr 1,000 bn to finance a three-year emergency plan to accelerate the country's economic growth. However, part of this programme was used to refinance a debt of $ 164 m owed by the 'Société Nationale de Raffinage'. In December, the AfDB approved a loan of € 24 m (CFAfr 15.7 bn) to the Kribi Power Development Corporation, to extend the gas power plant of Kribi. This project, 'Kribi II' was planned to add 125 MW, to bring the total capacity of the plant to 341 MW. It was supposed to address the energy deficit, estimated at 100 MW, while demand was believed to be growing grow annually by 8%. € 35 m or 25% of the cost would be paid by the shareholders (government and Globeleq). The rest would come from international donors (IFC, AfDB, EIB, the Netherlands Development Finance Company, Proparco and the 'Banque de Développement des Etats de l'Afrique Centrale') and national donors (Standard Chartered Bank Cameroon, Afriland First Bank, 'Société Commerciale de Banque Cameroon', 'Banque Internationale du Cameroun pour l'Epargne et le Crédit', and 'Société Générale Cameroun') that had supported 'Kribi I'.

All of these loans were seen as worrying by many analysts, who considered that Cameroon's medium-term economic health was threatened by a *high level of indebtedness*. Indeed, in a report on the economic prospects of Africa, the IMF calculated that Cameroon's debt had almost doubled in four years from 15% of GDP to just over 30%. The rating agency Fitch Ratings stated in December that, although the debt was still below the average in Africa, it had accelerated sharply in the last five years and that, although Cameroon's dependence on the oil sector was low (its hydrocarbon exports accounted for only 2% of its GDP), the amount of state investment projects appeared to be too high in proportion to its financing capacity. They also said that Cameroon remained dependent on Chinese loans and was trading less with its neighbours, and estimated that Cameroon was at the end of a political cycle, with many uncertainties about Biya's succession, reinforced by security issues.

Negotiations took place between the government and the two main *mobile phone operators*, the French group Orange and the South African MTN (which had 10 m subscribers and about 60% of the market), for the renewal of their licence, but the talks were difficult as the two operators wanted to reduce the price asked by the government (CFAfr 75 bn or € 114 m). They finally agreed on a renewal of their licences for 15 years, until February 2030. In addition, the government allowed the two firms to start offering third and fourth generation (3G and 4G) services. The third-largest mobile operator Nexttel, owned by Vietnam's Viettel Group, had received approval to offer 3G services when it was launched in 2014. According to statistical data, only 6% of Cameroon's population had Internet access, among the lowest rates in Africa, despite there being more than 16 m mobile phone subscribers.

Cameroon in 2016

The next presidential election, scheduled for 2018, was one of the main preoccupations of the majority of political players, who sought to discern the intentions of 83-year-old President Paul Biya, who had been in power since 1982. The atmosphere appeared increasingly tense within the presidential party, with some of its cadres advocating a change and others supporting the status quo incarnated by Biya. The latter faced two serious crises: a railway disaster involving the French corporate group Bolloré, and large-scale protest movement in the country's two English-speaking regions, which was still ongoing at the end of the year. The armed group Boko Haram continued to pose a substantial threat to security in the north, with implications for the agricultural sector and livestock farming. As a result of the drop in oil prices and the increase in military expenditure, the country's economic situation remained fragile, thus compelling the authorities to turn to the IMF, under pressure from France.

Domestic Politics

During much of the year, the political elite were on the lookout for any information about President Biya's plans regarding the *presidential election* scheduled for 2018. Cameroonians wondered whether the head of state would remain in office until the end of his mandate, whether he would again present himself as a candidate in 2018, whether he would call an early election, or whether he would change the constitution to create the office of a vice president, who would then become his potential successor. As the months passed, a renewal of his candidacy appeared increasingly likely. Though Biya, always a man of few words, did not personally comment on the subject, some of his close collaborators – including Martin Belinga Eboutou, director of the Civil Cabinet of the Presidency – spoke for

© KONINKLIJKE BRILL NV, LEIDEN, 2019 | DOI:10.1163/9789004401532_010

him: they launched public appeals calling for him to run again. The decisions taken within the presidential party, the 'Rassemblement Démocratique du Peuple Camerounais' (RDPC) were also a good indicator of Biya's intentions. The party was to organise its five-yearly congress in September, in compliance with the stipulations of its internal statutes to reappoint members of its executive bodies and choose its president, who would subsequently become its candidate for the next presidential election. Though repeatedly announced, the congress never convened: it was replaced in November by a simple meeting of the RDPC political bureau, which decided to adjourn the congress until an unspecified date, and most importantly to extend the duration of Biya's mandate as party president, which effectively made him RDPC candidate for the 2018 presidential election. This decision ensured that the dissensions within the RDPC would not be overly publicised and avoided any public dispute of Biya's mandate as president. In fact, the RDPC appeared increasingly divided over this issue: several of its cadres expressed their desire for change, while others opted for the status quo, fearing a fratricidal war and the loss of their privileges if Biya were to step down. The president's advanced age naturally played an increasingly important role in the reasoning of both groups: all political players were aware that, even if the head of state did not give the impression of wanting to hand over the reins, his years as president were becoming increasingly numbered. In October, a memorandum addressed to Biya and signed by leading members of the Mfoundi Division of the RPDC (equivalent to the political capital Yaoundé), indicated the frame of mind that prevailed among a number of cadres in his party: "Your power is becoming tribal and even familial" and the "Mfoundi and the peoples of the Great Centre and the East are the poor relations of your 35-year reign" were some of the formulations in this open letter, which also accused Biya of being "silent and dismissive". Even though other leaders of the Mfoundi expressed their disapproval following the publication of this text and gave him their support, the sense of unease remained strong.

An isolated incident, widely publicised on social media, came to illustrate the *end-of-reign mood* that prevailed within the presidential party and the country as a whole: on 20 May, the national day, one of the vehicles in Biya's cavalcade broke down in Yaoundé, on May 20 Boulevard, where the annual army parade was to take place under the eyes of the authorities and tight security. Soldiers of the presidential guard had to push the car in full view of an astounded public.

In late October, the authorities and Biya were subjected to strong criticism following the most serious *railway disaster* the country had ever experienced. Having been absent from Cameroon for a month, the president waited two days before deciding to return to Yaoundé – he was in Switzerland at the time. Though he decreed a national day of mourning, he did not visit the site of the tragedy, which occurred on 21 October in the town of Eséka, some 120 km from Yaoundé: a train belonging to Camrail (Cameroon Railways), more than 77% controlled by the French corporate group Bolloré, jumped the tracks. Travelling from Yaoundé to Douala, the country's economic capital, and carrying over 1,500 passengers, its journey ended brutally midway between the two cities. Several of its carriages broke loose and crashed into a ravine, killing at least 79 persons and injuring hundreds. A few hours earlier, the highway connecting Yaoundé and Douala had been literally cut in two following the rupture of a metal duct, which had been in bad state for a long time without any response from the relevant ministry. The network of secondary roads being barely developed, many travellers had opted for the train. In his traditional end-of-year speech on 31 December, the president promised that the in-depth inquiry that he had commissioned to investigate the disaster would uncover the truth. "I will take appropriate action, I have pledged myself to this," he added. However, many citizens doubted that those responsible for the disaster would ever stand trial, although there were numerous indications that the Bolloré group – which was omnipresent in several sectors of the Cameroonian economy and maintained direct ties to the presidential office – had committed several errors. Very soon after the accident, the media published documents and testimonies indicating the possibility that the train had been overloaded and that the majority of its carriages and its locomotive had a history of serious brake problems.

In the latter part of the year, the country also experienced a deep political crisis, the gravest since 2008, between the central power and the country's two *Anglophone regions*, the Southwest and the Northwest, home to 20% of the population. It all began as a simple corporatist mobilisation: English-speaking lawyers went on strike in mid-October, protesting against the lack of an English version of the basic legal texts of the Organisation for the Harmonisation of Business Law in Africa (OHADA) and the increasingly frequent application of the French-language civil code. (The two Anglophone regions that had made up former Southern Cameroon, administered by the British until the reunification of Cameroon in 1961, apply British common law, whereas the eight other regions, in which French is spoken, follow French civil law.) Day after day, the movement grew, in the absence of an adequate response on the part of the government. Students and teachers from the Southwest and the Northwest joined the strike, accusing the authorities of showing little consideration for their educational system. (The two Anglophone regions have also retained the British school system, evaluation methods and certifications, whereas the French-speaking regions adhere to the school system inherited from France.) From 21 November, classes were suspended at schools, colleges and universities in the Anglophone regions. Demonstrations also took place in a number of cities, notably in the most important ones: Buea and Bamenda. Little by little, the demands multiplied, some denouncing the marginalisation of the Anglophone regions in the sharing of power and resources, others calling for a return to federalism or even for the independence of Anglophone Cameroon. The Cameroonian flag was burned by demonstrators, while that of the Southern Cameroons National Council (SCNC), which had been demanding the independence of the Anglophone regions since 1995, was hoisted in front of the regional hospital in Bamenda.

Not unusually, the security forces reacted violently to the *demonstrations*, which led to serious clashes. According to the Social Democratic Front (SDF), the strongest opposition party, three persons died, although the government reported only one death. Several dozen persons, mostly young people, were arrested. There were various attempts at negotiation, notably by Prime Minister Philemon Yang, himself an Anglophone. In December, the head of government set up, among other things, a committee charged with investigating and proposing solutions to the concerns of the Anglophone lawyers. Deeming the government's propositions unsatisfactory, the protesters gradually organised themselves, creating the Cameroon Anglophone Civil Society Consortium (CACSC), an association of lawyers, teachers and members of civil society. While attempting to negotiate, the authorities also declared that they were categorically opposed to any revision of the state's institutional structure. In his end-of-year speech, President Biya insisted that "Cameroon is one and indivisible, and will remain so," accusing "a group of extremist, manipulated, and instrumentalised demonstrators" of trying to manipulate the masses. By late December, this conflict had not yet been resolved. The intelligence services suspected the members of the CACSC of having foreign supporters and of wanting to destabilise the state.

With regard to national security, the armed group *Boko Haram* remained a serious problem throughout the year in the Far North region, even though the actions attributed to it decreased in intensity and were essentially limited to suicide attacks. In January, no less than nine such attacks caused the death of more than 60 civilians. In February, 33 persons were killed and more than 100 injured in the wake of bomb explosions set off by two women during a funeral in Nguetchewe, a town located some 60 km from Maroua, and by two other women at a much used market in Meme, a village near Mora. In August and on Christmas Day, another five persons were killed and at least 34 injured by two more suicide attacks at markets in Mora. Boko Haram, officially operating from Nigeria and relying on a network of local collaborators, was said to have been responsible for the death of 1,500 persons since 2014. Within the framework of the Multinational Joint Task Force (MNJTF), the Cameroonian army crossed the border into Nigeria on a number of occasions. On 19 December, it conducted a raid on Nigerian territory in order to attack Boko Haram in one of its strongholds, some 20 km from the Cameroonian town of Achigachia. Roughly 8,500 soldiers were deployed in the region.

The *security forces* were again accused of *human rights violations*. According to AI, dozens of men, women and children accused of supporting Boko Haram were tortured by soldiers of the 'Brigade d'Intervention Rapide' (BIR), one of the army's elite units, on a military base situated near Maroua, as well as by government agents at the headquarters of the 'Direction Générale de la Recherche Extérieure' (DGRE), an intelligence service, in Yaoundé. Some of the detained persons died under torture, while others were reported missing. The International Organization for Migration (IOM) estimated that the number of persons displaced because of Boko Haram in the Far North had increased from 81,693 to 157,657 between April 2015 and July 2016.

Foreign Affairs

In keeping with his usual practice, President Biya attended very few African and international conferences. He did, however, travel to *Nigeria* on two occasions for official visits (on 2 and 15 May). In January, he welcomed the IMF director Christine Lagarde and he received Samantha Power, the US ambassador to the UN, on 19 April. The government continued to intensify its relations with *China*, Cameroon's most important economic partner. In July, Yaoundé and Beijing signed an agreement providing for the abolition of visa requirements for the holders of diplomatic or official passports from both countries.

Cameroon hosted several *international events*. In May, at Biya's request, the government organised an international conference on the theme 'Investing in Cameroon, Land of Attractiveness', with the aim of persuading investors to take an interest in the country. Several hundred participants attended this event, which was organised by Havas, a subsidiary of the Bolloré group. Manuel Barroso, former president of the European Commission, Donald Kaberuka, former president of the AfDB, and Pascal Lamy, former director-general of the WTO, were among the guests. In late November, Cameroon also hosted the 10th Africa Women's Cup of Nations, in which the national team, the Indomitable Lionesses, were defeated by the Super Falcons of Nigeria in the final. On 23 December, Yaoundé was host to an extraordinary CEMAC summit.

Earlier in the year, Cameroonian leaders, along with ordinary citizens, closely followed the presidential election in *Gabon* on 27 August and the post-electoral crisis that ensued. The majority of the Cameroonian media sided with the incumbent president Ali Bongo, and against his competitor Jean Ping. They believed that this crisis did not so much pitch Bongo against Ping but Bongo against France. In their opinion, Paris sought to remove Ali Bongo from power because a number of measures implemented by his government ran counter to the interests of several French companies. Anti-French slogans resurfaced in the Cameroonian media. According to a source close to the security forces, Biya had sent several hundred soldiers of the BIR to assist Bongo.

The crisis situations in the neighbouring *CAR* and in northern Nigeria continued to have humanitarian consequences for Cameroon: according to human rights organisations, the country was accommodating at least 276,000 CAR *refugees* in camps or host families in the south-western border region, often in difficult conditions. In addition, roughly 59,000 persons fleeing from Nigeria were housed in the Minawao camp, administered by the UN, in the Far

North region. Some 27,000 other refugees from Nigeria were also living outside this camp.

Socioeconomics Developments

The *budget* for 2016, which was designed to balance expenditure and revenue, was fixed at CFAfr 4,234.7 bn (€ 6.45 bn), an increase of CFAfr 488.1 bn (more than 13%) compared with 2015. At the end of the year, budgetary resources were estimated at CFAfr 4,218.4 bn, which included CFAfr 356 bn from oil revenues, CFAfr 1,590 bn in taxes and duties, CFAfr 695.9 bn in customs revenue, CFAfr 152 bn in non-fiscal revenue, and CFAfr 1,248.2 bn in loans and gifts. At the beginning of the year, the government banked on an economic growth of 6%, which ultimately turned out to be 5.6% – a drop of 0.2% compared with 2015. This shrinkage was mainly due to the slowdown in oil production (+3% in 2016, compared with +37% in 2015), or roughly 33 m barrels, and by the weakness in global crude oil prices and other raw materials. A portion of expenditure went into the execution of the construction projects for the Africa Cup of Nations, which took place at the end of year, and for the one the country would host in 2019. Part of the budget was, of course, used to finance the war effort against Boko Haram. According to a report published by the IMF in April, the budgetary impact of the increase in security costs amounted to somewhere between 1% and 2% of GDP between 2014 and 2015, in other words CFAfr 189 bn to CFAfr 378 bn (€ 287 m to € 575 m). The budget for 2016 was also marked by the implementation in August of the EPA with the EU – the monthly losses from this agreement having been evaluated at CFAfr 100 m by the Cameroonian authorities. In late August, the finance minister stated that Cameroon's public debt amounted to CFAfr 4,754 bn, or 27.3% of GDP.

With regard to borrowing, the state of Cameroon floated a *compulsory bond* of CFAfr 150 bn (€ 230 m) in late September, with an interest yield of 5.5%. The funds raised by this bond were to help finance the relaunch of the 'Société d'Expansion et de Modernisation de la Riziculture de Yagoua' (SEMRY) and the 'Société de Développement du Coton' (SODECOTON), a subsidiary of the French GEOCOTON, the expansion of the deep water port of Kribi, the motorway connecting Yaoundé and the international airport of Nsimalen, the enlargement of the Lom Pangar and Memve'ele dams, and a project to supply the capital and its surroundings with drinking water. This was the fourth compulsory bond issued by Cameroon since 2010. The first transaction, which had raised CFAfr 200 bn, had been fully reimbursed in December 2015, according to Finance Minister Alamine Ousmane Mey. In December, the World Bank granted a loan of $ 325 m to allow for the modernisation of the electricity network and to assist in the launching of the newly founded 'Société Nationale de Transport d'Électricité' (SONATREL), tasked, among other things, with the operation, maintenance and development of the public electricity distribution network and its interconnections with other networks. Roughly 74% of Cameroonians were living in areas directly connected to the electricity grid.

In the *agricultural sector* (which contributed approximately 22% of GDP), there was improvement in a number of sectors: cocoa exports increased by 38%, cotton by 31%, and bananas by 7%. The start of production on new plantations and the phytosanitary treatment of old groves explained the increase in cocoa production. However, the situation remained very difficult in the Far North due to Boko Haram raids: according to the Ministry of Agriculture, at least 4,500 ha of land were abandoned, and an investigation conducted by the Ministry of Livestock and Fisheries estimated that Boko Haram fighters had, over recent years, stolen or killed nearly 30,000 head of cattle and nearly 20,000 small ruminants in this region, and that their attacks had led to the closure of some 20 cattle markets, and thus of most the region's selling points. The exactions of Boko Haram also led to a significant decrease in fishing activities in the area of Lake Chad. In May, losses were estimated at nearly

CFAfr 55 bn (€ 83.8 m) in the livestock sector and CFAfr 8.5 bn (nearly € 13 m) in the fishing sector. At least 135 cattle farmers were killed. Estimates revealed that the economy of the area most affected by the raids of Boko Haram contributed no more than 5% of GDP, as compared with 7.3% before the appearance of the armed group. Income losses on the national level were said to amount to roughly € 686 m per year, or € 2 bn, since 2014.

Elsewhere in the country, *poultry farming* also suffered significant losses due to an outbreak of avian flu. The epidemic was first detected in May in Yaoundé, before spreading to several other regions, including the West, where 80% of the country's poultry production was concentrated. Tens of thousands of birds had to be slaughtered and the sale of poultry was banned for several weeks. The 'Interprofession Avicole du Cameroun' (IPAVIC) producers' association, which had expected a production of 50 m broiler chickens for the year, had to revise this figure downwards to 30 m. Members of civil society and cattle farmers protested on several occasions against the measures taken by the government, deeming them to be disproportionate and inappropriate. Some even suspected ill-intentioned economic players, in complicity with certain administrative authorities, of attempting to weaken the national poultry sector to benefit poultry importers.

With regard to large enterprises, a plan for the restructuring of the national airline Cameroon Airlines Corporation (Camair-Co) was adopted. It provided for the clearing of Camair-Co's CFAfr 35 bn debt, the purchase of nine additional aircraft, and the opening of new national and international air routes. A new management team was also appointed in August.

The level of *corruption* remained high. 'Opération Epervier', launched in 2006 by President Biya to combat corruption, did not appear to make any progress. One of its most famous victims, Jean Marie Atangana Mebara, was again condemned by a Special Criminal Court on 23 June: he was sentenced to 25 years' imprisonment for the embezzlement in 2003 of nearly CFAfr 3 bn (€ 4.4 m) earmarked for the purchase of a presidential airplane. Atangana Mebara had already received two sentences of 20 years and 15 years in prison for other misappropriations of funds. His supporters continued to denounce the judicial system as being instrumentalised for political purposes. For part of the year, one scandal in particular was widely commented on by the media: a case of misappropriated funds within the 'Banque Internationale du Cameroun pour l'Épargne et le Crédit' (BICEC), a subsidiary of the French group 'Banque Populaire-Caisse d'Épargne' (BPCE) and Cameroon's most important banking network. Senior Cameroonian managers of the bank were imprisoned on charges of embezzling tens of millions of euros over a period of more than ten years. This affair raised many questions among both experts and Cameroonian citizens: many asked themselves how these misappropriations could have gone on for so many years without being detected by successive directors and those responsible for internal audits within the BICEC, all of them French. The National Anti-Corruption Commission (CONAC) celebrated the tenth anniversary of its founding. CONAC announced that it had recovered nearly CFAfr 6 bn (€ 9 m) since its inception and had received 3,268 accusations of corruption in 2015, compared with only 168 in 2008. CONAC also published two reports in the course of the year. The first showed, in particular, that the compensation fund for the victims of the 'Nsam fire disaster' (when an oil depot located in Yaoundé had exploded in 1998, officially causing the death of 250 persons) had been the target of embezzlements amounting to more than CFAfr 14 bn (€ 21 m). The same report also revealed that several ministries, including those of justice, defence, foreign relations, communication, the supreme state audit, and the delegate general for national security had not implemented the National Anti-Corruption Strategy, despite its having been approved by the government and the country's technical and financial partners in February 2011. The second CONAC report showed that the state had lost more than CFAfr 171 bn (€ 260 m) through corruption in 2015. The detected infractions included the failure of the cell phone providers (Orange Cameroun, MTN Cameroon and Camtel) to pay their taxes and duties.

A number of changes were made to the justice system: in June, parliament adopted a *new penal code*, the preceding one having not been revised since 1967. Certain paragraphs in this legislation, which was enacted by Biya on 12 July, were nevertheless heavily criticised by civil rights organisations and opposition groups: the latter were shocked by the fact that adultery, vagrancy and begging were now punishable by imprisonment. Civil rights organisations also deplored the fact that tenants who failed to pay their rent for more than two months could now be sentenced to as much as three years in prison, even though approximately one-third of the country's households were in rented accommodation and nearly half of Cameroonians lived below the poverty threshold. In addition, homosexuality was still a punishable offence and the death penalty was retained. The new code also introduced a system of community work and restorative justice that was meant to reduce the number of short prison sentences. Initially, the text submitted to the vote of the deputies included a provision conferring immunity on sitting cabinet ministers, but protests were so strong that this section of the code had to be removed.

Cameroon in 2017

The crisis between the government and the country's two English-speaking regions that had begun in late 2016 worsened over the months and turned into an armed conflict involving guerilla attacks on the security forces. These acts of violence became President Paul Biya's main problem as he appeared to be preparing to run for the presidential election of 2018. In the northern part of the country, the militant group Boko Haram continued its sporadic attacks against the civilian population. On the economic front, oil production declined. Though less affected by the fall in commodity prices than the other countries in the region thanks to the diversification of its economy, Cameroon was forced to conclude a loan agreement with the IMF.

Domestic Politics

The crisis that had set the government and the country's two English-speaking regions – the Southwest and the Northwest – in opposition since 2016 gradually worsened over the months. While the authorities refused to return to the federalism demanded by the anglophone leaders, they did agree to open negotiations. These talks led to the creation, in late June, of a *National Commission for the Promotion of Bilingualism and Multiculturalism*, then, in February, to the suspension of a strike call issued by several teachers' trade unions, and finally to a resumption of classes in certain schools in the two regions in question. Just as it was holding talks, however, the government declared two organisations illegal: the Cameroon Anglophone Civil Society Consortium, established in December 2016 as an association of lawyers, teachers, and members of the English-speaking civil society, and the Southern Cameroons National Council, a political party that had been calling for the independence of

© KONINKLIJKE BRILL NV, LEIDEN, 2019 | DOI:10.1163/9789004401532_011

the English-speaking regions since 1995. The authorities also asked Internet access providers to suspend their services in the two crisis areas from 17 January onward, as they feared that online social networks could be used to encourage and organise protest movements. This radical decision had an adverse effect: it increased the tensions and the resentment of the English-speaking minority, roughly 20% of the total population, against the central government. It also focused the attention of the international media on Cameroon. The American whistleblower Edward Snowden was one of those who spread the hashtag #BringBackOurInternet, which was widely used in social network news feeds. The suspension measure was not lifted until 20 April, at the demand of President Biya.

In the meantime, activists campaigning for the anglophone cause had, in early March, announced the creation of a new movement named Southern Cameroons/Ambazonia Consortium United Front, which presented itself as "a broad-based movement that unites all organisations which seek the restoration of the statehood of Southern Cameroons", i.e. the former English-speaking Cameroon.

The second half of the year was marked by *outbreaks of violence*. In August, private and public schools in Southwest and Northwest were set on fire by alleged supporters of the secession of both regions. In late August, only a few days before the beginning of the school year, the government attempted to calm things down by ordering the release of some 70 leaders and activists of the anglophone cause who had been arrested in late 2016. Classes were able to begin but some schools remained closed in Southwest and Northwest, while a number of parents were threatened with reprisals if they sent their children to school.

On 1 October, the anniversary of the official reunification of the English and French-speaking parts of Cameroon, radicals defied the authority of Yaoundé: they 'proclaimed' the birth of a state called *Ambazonia*, corresponding to the former English-speaking Cameroon. This led to renewed demonstrations: for instance, between 30,000 and 50,000 people demonstrated in Bamenda, the capital of Northwest Region, where the government had deployed a large number of security personnel. This first day of October was marked by heavy violence: human rights organisations claimed that 17 persons were killed in clashes between demonstrators and police. According to the local UNHCR Office, these events forced more than 3,000 people to flee to neighbouring Nigeria.

Condemning the violence and calling for dialogue, President Biya, in the days that followed, dispatched the English-speaking Prime Minister Philemon Yang to Bamenda in an attempt to revive talks. But to no avail: in November, the crisis turned into an armed conflict. Three gendarmes and one soldier were killed in attacks by separatists in Southwest and Northwest. Improvised bombs also exploded in Bamenda, including one in the vicinity of the Mobile Intervention Group, a police unit comprising the largest contingent of policemen in the region. There were no casualties, but a curfew was immediately imposed in Bamenda. Access to the Internet again became difficult in Southwest and Northwest.

Furthermore, a number of media also reported that the government had issued *international arrest warrants* against some ten secessionists, including members of the Southern Cameroons Ambazonian Governing Council, a kind of unity government. The most militant secessionists, of whom at least some lived abroad, made extensive use of online social networks to communicate and, in particular, to explain that the police and gendarmes deployed in their regions constituted "colonial forces" of occupation which must be resisted by force of arms. Pictures of men in uniform also circulated, the latter being presented as members of the Ambazonia Defence Forces commanded by Ayaba Cho Lucas. Over the months, the militants of the anglophone cause appeared increasingly divided and split into three groups: those calling for more justice but not challenging the institutional organisation of the state, those advocating a return to federalism, and those actively militating in favour of secession. A number of political players estimated that the government, by stepping up its military presence in the two English-speaking regions and having 'moderate' leaders arrested, had only strengthened the most extremist fringe groups.

Between late November and late December, the separatists mounted new *attacks against members of the security forces*. On 1 December, Biya blamed "a band of terrorists claiming to be part of a secessionist movement" and announced that all steps would be taken "to end these criminals' ability to do harm". Immediately afterwards, the Rapid Intervention Battalion, an elite army unit reporting directly to the president and known for its ruthless methods, was deployed to Manyu division, where the attacks were concentrated. In the following days, its soldiers made at least one incursion into Nigeria, where some of the secessionist fighters had a rear base. The military authorities also intensified the surveillance of the railway line connecting Yaoundé to the northern city of Ngaoundéré, as it feared that anglophone 'separatists' might attempt to carry out acts of sabotage. By late December, nearly 20 members of the security forces had been assassinated in the space of two months. In his end-of-year speech, President Biya again took a firm stand, reiterating his resolve that all those who had taken up arms "should be fought relentlessly and held accountable for their crimes before the courts of law".

Even though the 'anglophone crisis' dominated the news and ranked prominently in the concerns of many Cameroonians, it was never debated in the *National Assembly*. This remained so until late November, when a scheduled plenary review of the draft budget law for 1918 was interrupted by deputies of the Social Democratic Front (SDF), the main opposition party that had been founded in 1990 in Bamenda, who called for a debate on the issue. Their colleagues from the presidential party, the Cameroon People's Democratic Movement, expressed their opposition to this idea by walking out of the plenary assembly, while the parliamentarians of the SDF sang a song hostile to President Biya. On 11 December, the deputies of the SDF again prevented the Assembly from carrying out its work – this time by using vuvuzelas to make themselves heard, but to no avail.

As the anglophone crisis grew in intensity, the armed group *Boko Haram* remained active in the north, mounting sporadic attacks against civilians. In late September, eight persons were killed by a suicide bomber in the village of Ouro-Kessoum, 2 km from the Nigerian border, in Far North Region. One month later, 11 more people had their throats cut in Gouderi, while a suicide attack carried out by a young girl resulted in the death of five children in Zamga, 2 km from the border. A UNICEF report published in April stated that 27 children had been forced to carry out suicide attacks in the region between January and March, compared with nine in the corresponding period of 2016. Since 2014, according to the NGO International Crisis Group (ICG), Boko Haram was believed to have killed 2,000 civilians and soldiers, and to have kidnapped 1,000 persons in Far North Region. In September, HRW, for its part, accused the Cameroonian authorities of having forcibly deported 4,000 refugees to Nigeria in the course of the year, on suspicion of being linked to Boko Haram. The UNHCR also condemned these deportations as a violation of the agreements signed by Cameroon within the framework of the protection of refugees. The Cameroonian government dismissed all these charges. In July, it also issued a protest following the publication of a report by AI that, as in the previous year, accused the security forces of having committed war crimes and acts of torture in the context of the war against Boko Haram.

The *presidential election* scheduled for October 2018 was regularly brought up for discussion throughout the year. President Biya, aged 84 and in power for 35 years, gave no clear indication of his intentions, but the probability that he would run for the presidency was deemed to be high: in two speeches, he thus referred to an event planned for 2019 as if it were clear that he would still be in charge at that time. Although the 'anglophone crisis' was never debated in the National Assembly, it was used as an argument by those who wished to see him step down from power as well as by those who supported him. For the former group, this conflict – like the one involving Boko Haram – demonstrated that Biya, whom his party had long presented as a guarantor of peace, had become a destabilising factor and that it was time for him to step down. The president of the Episcopal Conference of Cameroon, Archbishop Samuel Kléda, also issued a statement to this effect at year's end. For the second group, Biya was still the right man for the job: active in the corridors of political power since 1962, he was, according to them, the one who was best qualified to come to terms with the country's complexity, having succeeded in containing Boko Haram within a confined area. On the opposition side, a number of personalities expressed their readiness to run for the presidency, including the lawyer Akere Muna, a native of Northwest and the son of the former prime minister Solomon Tandeng Muna, the jurist Maurice Kamto, president of the Cameroon Renaissance Movement and former minister-delegate to the minister of justice, and the agronomist and civil society activist Bernard Njonga. The SDF, for its part, did not disclose its plans: it remained unclear whether its chairman, John Fru Ndi, would run at all, having already been a candidate in 1992, 2004 and 2011.

One of the rare positive events of the year for Cameroon, the victory of the national football team (the Indomitable Lions) at the *Africa Cup of Nations* ('Coupe d'Afrique des Nations'; CAN) on 5 February was able to revive the feeling of belonging to a united country, though only for a few days. After winning the trophy, the goalkeeper Fabrice Ondoa, hero of this CAN and a French-speaking native of Yaoundé, proclaimed first in French and then in English, and in explicit reference to the anglophone crisis: "It is thanks to our unity that we were able to achieve this (sentence originally in French) ... My brothers, I am from Bamenda. Bamenda, I love you!"

Foreign Affairs

With regard to Cameroonian diplomacy, the year witnessed an extensive shift of personnel which, in early November, affected the central administration and many of the country's diplomatic missions abroad. These changes had been expected to take place for many years. The media noted that they occurred in a context in which *Canada and Great Britain* had asked Yaoundé to recall the Cameroonian diplomats serving in those countries, where they were accused of engaging in activities inconsistent with their status.

President Biya's foreign policy was largely concerned with the anglophone crisis. On 25 November, he thus dispatched Minister of Territorial Administration and Decentralisation Emmanuel René Sadi to *Nigeria* with a "special message" for President Muhammadu Buhari. Sadi was received by Vice President Yemi Osinbajo. A few weeks earlier, thousands of Cameroonians from Northwest and Southwest Regions had crossed the border to seek refuge in Cross River State in south-eastern Nigeria. On 7 December, President Biya then received the high commissioner of Nigeria to Cameroon, Lawan Abba Gashagar, again to discuss the anglophone crisis.

The conflict in the English-speaking regions was also the subject of several statements on the part of Cameroon's Western partners. In July, on the occasion of the French national holiday, the ambassador of *France* to Cameroon addressed it in a speech in which he advocated dialogue. UN Secretary-General António Guterres, for his part, asked the Cameroonian authorities to conduct an investigation into the acts of violence that had taken place on 1 October. In late October, after visiting the CAR, Guterres made a brief stop in Yaoundé, where he met with Biya, although the subject of their conversation was not made public. In November, furthermore, the UN Regional Office for Central Africa (UNOCA) declared that it was "particularly concerned by the upsurge of violence, especially against the civilian population and state agents" in the English-speaking regions. It reiterated the commitment of the UN to the territorial integrity and unity of Cameroon and invited the various parties to resolve their differences through peaceful means. In late December, Patricia Scotland, secretary-general of the Commonwealth, of which Cameroon is a member, paid a four-day visit to the country. She met with the country's main political leaders as well as with representatives of the political parties, civil society and the business community. She attended an official diner with President Biya, at which she expressed her "great sadness" over the events in the English-speaking regions. She also called upon Cameroonians to "preserve peace and unity, and to encourage in all circumstances genuine dialogue."

In late October, after the publication of an *ICG* report on the anglophone crisis, the government announced that it was barring the ICG from conducting activities on its territory. Minister of Communication Issa Tchiroma Bakary accused the ICG of being a "destabilization organization defending the interests of the secessionist movements veiled with unconfessed interests whose sole dream is to install chaos" in Cameroon.

Two cases pertaining to *freedom of speech* were also widely commented on abroad, especially in France. They both came to a close at year's end. The first involved the journalist Ahmed Abba, a Hausa-speaking correspondent of the French public radio station Radio France Internationale (RFI): he was released on 22 December after spending 29 months in pretrial detention. In 2016, he had been sentenced in the first instance to ten years' imprisonment for condoning acts of terrorism. Having appealed against this verdict, he was finally acquitted by the military tribunal of Yaoundé but sentenced to 24 months' imprisonment for "non-denunciation of terrorism". The management of RFI, which operates under the auspices of the French Ministry of Foreign Affairs, became very active in this matter, which in turn generated considerable tension with the government. In December, the American-Cameroonian writer Patrice Nganang was arrested and imprisoned for three weeks before being released and deported to the United States. He was prosecuted for "apology for crime" and for posting "threats" on Facebook, where he said that he would like to "put a bullet right in Paul Biya's forehead".

As in previous years, the security situation remained poor on the border with the *CAR*. In July, the Cameroonian authorities decided to close the border for several weeks due to clashes between armed groups in the CAR. On 11 September, presumed rebels from this neighbouring country led an incursion into the territorial department of Boumba-et-Ngoko, 58 km from the city of Yokadouma. These armed men assaulted the employees and ransacked the equipment of a French logging company, the 'Compagnie Forestière du Cameroun'. Disturbances also occurred on the border with Equatorial Guinea: in late December, the Cameroonian police detained some 30 persons transporting arms and military uniforms who were about to cross the border, coming from the city of Kye-Ossi. The military security service and the local police in Ebolowa opened an investigation into this matter.

Not accustomed to taking part in regional or continental events, President Biya nevertheless attended the 5th AU-EU Summit in Côte d'Ivoire in late November. One month earlier, he had travelled to Chad to attend an extraordinary CEMAC summit.

Socioeconomic Developments

Balanced in terms of expenditure and revenue, the fiscal *budget* for the year amounted to CFAfr 4373.8 bn (€ 6.6 bn), 3.3% higher than the budget for 2016. Domestic assets amounted to CFAf 3143.3 bn (71.8% of the total amount, an increase of 9.6% over the current fiscal year), while the external assets (loans and donations) were estimated at CFAfr 625 bn. Remaining cautious in its calculations, the government banked on an oil price of $ 40 per barrel and hoped to take CFAfr 495.1 bn in oil revenues, an increase of 12% over 2016. To improve its fiscal revenues, Yaoundé also relied on the increase of a special tax on oil products and on the reintroduction of customs duties on non-pulverised cement (clinker). These duties had been suspended in 2009 in order to combat the high cost of living following the sociopolitical unrest of February 2008. At the time, only one cement factory was in operation, the 'Cimenteries du Cameroun' (Cimencam), compared with four in 2017. The other suspensions of customs duties that had been agreed in 2008 (notably on imported wheat) were maintained. With regard to non-tax revenues, the state hoped to raise CFAfr 1297 bn, including CFAfr 585 bn in loans from development partners, CFAfr 560 bn raised on the financial markets, and CFAfr 85 bn from donations. On the expenditure side, the budget earmarked 47.1% of total expenditure for the functioning of the state and 36.3% for investments (an increase of 4% over the previous budget).

The government reckoned on an *economic growth* of 6% and an inflation rate of 3.3%. These predictions exceeded those of the IMF, which expected a growth of 4.2% and an inflation rate of 2.2%. According to the IMF, it was actually 3.6%. This growth was driven by ongoing infrastructural projects. However, the implementation of these large projects was necessarily linked to increased import needs, so that the trade balance remained in deficit.

At the end of the year, the 'Société Nationale des Hydrocarbures' (SNH) announced that Cameroon had sold 16.9 m barrels of *crude oil*, compared with 20.5 m in 2016. According to the state-owned corporation, this decrease was due to the decline in domestic production, which amounted to 28 m barrels by the end of the year, down 16.4% from 2016. While production was mainly from offshore fields located in the coastal drainage basins (Rio del Rey and Douala/Kribi Campo), the SNH hoped that mapping the largely unexplored areas on the mainland would lead to the discovery of new oil reserves. In June, it accordingly initiated a procedure to map the sedimentary basins in Southwest (Mamfe) and North (Garoua/Koum). It also signed a contract with the American company Noble Energy, in which it agreed to share 4 bn m^3 of natural gas and 18 m barrels of gas condensates in Cameroon's Yoyo Block, located in the Douala/Kribi Campo basin. The exploitation of natural gas reserves could partly compensate for the projected fall in oil revenues. The production of natural gas was on the rise anyway, reaching 335 m m^3 on 31 October, which represented an increase of 15.5% compared with the same period in 2016. It was expected to reach 445.1 m m^3 by the end of the year.

The 'anglophone crisis' had an economic impact that was still difficult to assess at year's end. The *suspension of Internet services* in Southwest and Northwest Regions proved costly for local businesses, especially in Buea. Businesses operating in the field of new technologies were forced to relocate to Douala in order to continue their activities. On the whole, economic activity was sluggish all year round in these two regions. In addition, it became apparent that the disturbances had the effect of increasing the fraudulent exports of cocoa to Nigeria.

In June, following the conference of the heads of state of CEMAC, held in Yaoundé in December 2016, the government and the IMF agreed on an economic programme supported by an ECF of $ 666.2 m. A few months later, in September, the deputy managing director of the IMF visited Yaoundé. He stated that the economic health of Cameroon was relatively better than that of its neighbours but contended that the pre-crisis levels of economic growth were unsustainable. He explained that it was necessary to reduce government spending by focusing on the elimination of wasteful or superfluous expenditure. He assured everyone that the salaries of civil servants would not be lowered and that spending would be increased in the health and education sectors. He advocated a reduction of administrative formalities, a simplification of the fiscal system, and greater participation of the private sector in the main sectors of the economy. He also announced that the services of the IMF would offer assistance in the field of revenue administration, the modernisation of taxes and customs, budget management, and budget risk management.

There was modest progress in the realisation of *construction projects* aimed at creating new infrastructure: at year's end, a new bridge over the River Wouri was opened to traffic in Douala, thereby reducing the road traffic problems that had been having a crippling effect on the economic capital. The deep-water port of Kribi, on the other hand, was not put into service, and the work to improve the condition of the road connecting Douala and Yaoundé was interrupted. In December, the AfDB granted Cameroon a loan of € 150 m for the construction of the Nachtigal hydroelectric dam, with a production capacity of 420 MW. Located 65 km to the north of Yaoundé, on the Sanaga River, this power plant should boost Cameroon's power production capacity by 30%. Expected to cost € 1.1 bn, the dam would be built by the Nachtigal Hydro Power Company, a joint venture of the Cameroonian state (40%), the 'Electricité de France" Group (40%) and the International Finance Corporation, a subsidiary of the World Bank (30%). Construction would begin in 2018, and the dam was scheduled to become operational in 2022. In 2015, the *electricity* generation capacity of Cameroon, with one of the highest potentials in Africa in terms of electric energy, was estimated at 1,289 MW, with hydroelectric energy representing 59% of the total. Roughly 48% of the Cameroonian population had access to electricity. In late October, the American Hydromine Company announced that it planned to invest $ 3 bn (CFAfr 1,500 bn) in the construction of the Grand Eweng hydroelectric dam, also to be located on the Sanaga River, near the villages of Kan, in the territorial department of Sanaga Maritime, and Dibang, in Nyong-et-Kéllé. This dam (1,800 MW) could be finished by 2025. Hydromine would carry out this project with private funding. On 26 October, the governor of Centre Region and the managing director of the Hydromine branch office in Cameroon began marking out the construction site in Dibang.

There were no changes in the *mining* sector. However, an NGO called 'Forêts et Développement Rural' (FODER) implicated Chinese mining companies in numerous accidents that occurred at open mining sites in East Region, claiming that 43 persons died in 2017 as a result of landslides. The mining companies were accused of not protecting the sites they had exploited, leaving them open to ill-equipped local craftspeople working without any kind of safety precautions. Between 2012 and 2014, according to FODER, 250 mining sites were thus opened and not protected by 65 different companies in East Region, known for its rich gold deposits.

In May, President Biya surprised everyone by publishing the conclusions of the administrative commission of inquiry that had been set up in the immediate aftermath of the *Camrail train accident* of 21 October 2016, which officially claimed the lives of 79 people and injured at least 600, in addition to an undetermined number of disappearances. The fact that Camrail is a subsidiary of the French Bolloré Group, omnipresent in Cameroun and often considered to be all-powerful, had led many to believe that the authorities would prudently set the issue aside until it was forgotten. The commission established that "the responsibility for the derailment of the Intercity train no. 152", which connected Yaoundé and Douala, "lay mainly with the rail carrier, the Camrail company". The causes of the accident, which occurred in the small town of Eséka, were determined to have been "excessive speed (96 km/h)", "non-compliance with certain safety rules", "severe anomalies and defects" and "use of passenger cars with partly defective brake elements". The presidency, which had until then always protected the interests of the French industrial group, announced that it had requested an audit of the concession contract signed by Cameroon and Camrail in 1999. According to experts, the terms of this agreement were particularly unfavourable to the state and created the conditions that led to the accident.